ASTRONOMY

ASTRONOMY: THE SCIENTIFIC STUDY OF CELESTIAL BODIES.

Date:	Experiment:	Notes:

1 The Sun and Us

See the relationship between the Sun, Earth, and the Moon.

Materials
- one large balloon
- modeling clay
- wire
- string
- plastic bottle
- drinking straw

Did You Know?

Without the Sun there would be no life on Earth. The Sun provides light, warmth, and energy. The Sun is much bigger than any of the planets in our solar system. In fact, compared to Earth, the Sun is 100 times bigger in diameter, 330,000 times heavier, and a million times bigger in volume.

STEPS

1. Loop one end of a piece of wire around the neck of the plastic bottle. The wire should be secure but not so tight that it can't spin around the bottle.

2. Blow up a large balloon (Sun) as big as possible and attach it to the neck of the bottle.

3. Make two round balls with the modeling clay—one about the size of a ping pong ball (Earth) and the other a little smaller in size than a small marble (Moon).

4. Push the straw through the middle of the larger ball until it sits halfway down the straw. Then slide the straw over the end of the wire, stopping once the tip of the wire is visible at the top of the straw.

5. Bend the wire at the bottom end of the straw, so it is tilted on approximately a 45 degree angle.

6. Slide another piece of wire inside the straw, leaving approximately 2½ in (6 cm) sticking out the top of the straw.

7. Slide the smaller ball onto the end of this wire, then curve the wire so the smaller ball sits about 1¼ in (3 cm) from Earth. Both balls should be at roughly the same height.

8. Spin the wires to show how the Sun, Earth, and Moon move in relation to each other.

2 Gravity

Experience the pull of gravity.

Materials
- elastic
- ball or balloon

Did You Know?
The planets in our solar system are kept in place by gravity. The farther the planet is from the Sun the longer it takes to orbit (travel) around the Sun. One trip around the Sun is equal to a year.

STEPS

1. Whirl a ball or balloon on the end of a piece of elastic.
2. The stretch of the elastic represents the gravitational pull of the Sun.

---

3 Gravity Pulls

Explore the force of gravity.

Materials
- lead sinker
- ball
- jug
- books

Did You Know?
Gravity makes all things on Earth stay on Earth. If gravity did not exist you and I, tables, chairs, food, and everything would be floating around in space! Gravity also keeps the planets and the stars of the Milky Way in their place! Gravity acts in the same way on objects of differing size and weight.

STEPS

1. Prop a table up by placing some books under one end of it—about 2 in (6 cm).
2. Observe the speed of the ball as it rolls down the table.
3. Throw a ball into the air and observe its path.
4. Pour water from the jug and again observe its path.
5. The paths of these objects are called parabolic.
6. Now drop the lead sinker and the ball. Observe the difference.

4 Making Gravity

Make your own gravity.

Materials
- small can
- string
- water

STEPS
1. Attach a piece of string to a small can.
2. Half fill the can with water.
3. Do not put the lid back on.
4. In an outside area, swing the can around your head very quickly.

Did You Know?
The surface gravity on the planets in our solar system varies. If Earth has a surface gravity of one, the surface gravity on the other planets would be as follows:

Mercury: 0.38	Venus: 0.91
Mars: 0.38	Jupiter: 2.36
Saturn: 0.92	Uranus: 0.89
Neptune: 1.12	Pluto*: 0.07

*Dwarf planet

---

5 Down with Gravity

Experiment with weight and the force of gravity.

Materials
- newspaper
- 2 oranges
- chair
- grape

I know this looks like a recipe for fruit salad ... but it is definitely an experiment on gravity.

STEPS
1. Place newspaper on the floor.
2. Place a chair on top of the newspaper.
3. Carefully stand on the seat of the chair.
4. Holding one orange in each hand, extend your arms. Each orange must be at the same height.
5. Let the oranges go at the same time and observe which one lands first.
6. Repeat from step 3 but this time hold an orange in one hand and a grape in the other.
7. Observe which one lands first.

Did You Know?
The force on Earth that pulls everything down is called gravity. No matter how much an object weighs, gravity pulls it downward at the same speed.

6 See Inside a Box

Can you see inside a closed box without removing the lid?

STEPS

1. Put the object inside the box and close the lid.
2. Stick the piece of paper to the top of the lid.
3. Use your knitting needle to gently poke through the lid of the box.
4. You will need to measure how far your knitting needle goes into the box before it hits something. Measure the knitting needle and use a different color for each measurement, then record this on the paper on top of the box.
5. When you have done this across the whole lid of the box you will see a shape start to emerge.
6. Using the heights you have recorded you will be able to get a 3D idea of the object.

Materials
- a large box with a lid
- an object (teddy bear, plastic bottle)
- knitting needle or skewer
- a piece of paper

Did You Know?

Scientists use radar to look at Earth's surface when clouds cover it. Radar uses light energy but we can't see it. The radar bounces off surfaces and makes echoes that the radar antenna can hear.

---

7 The Shape of Earth

Replicate the shape of Earth.

STEPS

1. Fill the balloon with water and tie the balloon with string.
2. Put a screw eye into your hand drill where the drill bit normally goes.
3. Tie the balloon to the screw eye using the other end of the string.
4. Go outside or to a sink and start to turn the handle of the drill.
5. Gradually add more speed.

Materials
- balloon
- water
- string
- hand drill
- screw eye

Did You Know?

The shape you have just made is an oblate spheroid. Earth also has this shape, although not quite as extreme as your balloon's shape.

8 Day and Night

Simulate day and night.

STEPS

1. Draw the shapes of Australia and North America on the paper. Cut them out and tape them onto the balloon in their global positions.
2. Tie the balloon so it is freely hanging.
3. Shine a flashlight onto one side of the balloon. Open the chute and let it fall from the same height as you did the paper.
4. Slowly turn the balloon.
5. Try holding the balloon to show these times in Australia or the USA:
   - midnight
   - sunrise
   - midday
   - sunset.

Materials
- piece of string
- balloon
- paper and pen
- scissors
- tape

Did You Know?

Earth is like a giant ball spinning in the darkness of space. Earth is always moving and takes 24 hours to spin on its axis. When one side of Earth is facing the Sun it is experiencing day time, while on the other side it is experiencing night time.

9 Observing Night and Day

Experience the differences between night time and day time.

STEPS

1. Find a spot that you are able to get to during different times of the day and night (sunrise, sunset, midday, and just before bed are the best times).
2. At the above times go to the chosen spot and observe.
3. Look for things such as differences or similarities in what you see and feel. Look out for animals and birds, people, the temperature, etc.

Materials
- pencil
- clipboard
- paper

Did You Know?

There are many animals that are nocturnal. This means that they sleep during the day and come out during the night. Some examples of nocturnal animals are possums and owls. Many people also sleep during the day and work at night. Some examples are doctors and police officers.

10 Seasons

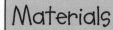

See how Earth experiences the different seasons.

STEPS

1. Slowly spin Earth around.
2. Sit Earth onto the bowl so the line of the equator is slightly sloping.
3. Rest the flashlight onto the books so it is shining just above the equator. Where the Sun's light is brightest, the countries will be experiencing summer. Where the Sun's light is farthest away, the countries will be experiencing winter.

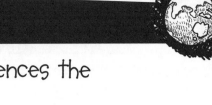

Materials
- balloon with a line drawn around the middle (Earth and its equator)
- bowl (to rest Earth on)
- flashlight (the Sun)
- books (to rest the flashlight on)

Did You Know?
Light from the Sun does not fall evenly onto Earth because our planet is round. The equator is the hottest part of our planet because it is closest to the Sun and therefore it is where the Sun's light and heat are the strongest.

11 The Tides

Why does the ocean have high and low tides?

Is the tide coming in ... or going out? Depends where the moon is I suppose, but a nice day at the beach nevertheless!

STEPS

1. Half fill the bucket with water.
2. Place the ball in the bucket so it is floating.
3. Place both hands onto the ball and push down very slowly.
4. Let the ball come up again.
5. Watch the change in water level.

Materials
- bucket
- plastic ball or balloon
- water

Did You Know?
Seventy percent of Earth's surface is covered with oceans. Every twelve hours the tides rise and fall. This happens without the level of water changing. As Earth and the Moon spin, gravity pulls them together and the Moon pulls at the ocean water directly beneath it, causing it to rise and fall.

12 Angled Light

Why is it hotter at the Earth's equator?

STEPS

1. Turn the lights off in a room.
2. Put your piece of white paper on a table and aim the flashlight straight down at the paper. Note what you see.
3. Now tilt your flashlight and aim it at the paper. Note what you see now.

Materials
- flashlight
- white paper

Did You Know?

When the Sun shines on Earth at the equator, it is more intense, just like the flashlight facing straight down. When you move away from the equator the climate cools down because the light is on an angle.

---

13 Creating an Eclipse

Create an eclipse.

Materials
- tennis ball
- ping pong or table tennis ball
- flashlight
- table (with a table cloth)

STEPS

1. Place the tennis ball about 24 in (60 cm) from the flashlight and the ping pong ball between them (so the ping pong ball should be about 12 in (30 cm) from each object). Then make the room dark.
2. Shine the flashlight onto the tennis ball and move the ping pong ball around the tennis ball.
3. The tennis ball represents Earth, the ping pong ball represents the Moon, and the flashlight represents the Sun.
4. See what happens when the ping pong ball moves between the flashlight and the tennis ball and when it moves behind the tennis ball.

Did You Know?

Long ago, Chinese people used to think that a solar eclipse was a dragon swallowing the Sun. They would make noise by banging on drums and yelling to try to scare the dragon away. Of course, because solar eclipses are only temporary the Sun would always return.

14 Images of the Sun

View images of the Sun safely.

Did You Know?

Scientists and astronomers call the super, super hot gas in the Sun plasma, and its wispy atmosphere the corona. Sunstorms can occur when plasma explodes and escapes through the corona. We are safe on Earth, but satellites have been destroyed by sunstorms!
Warning: Never stare directly at the Sun as it will cause damage to your eyes.

Bud, a telecommunications satellite, survives a nasty sunstorm.

Materials
- binoculars
- books
- mirror
- window and wall opposite to one another

STEPS

1. Place the binoculars on some books facing out of a window so they are catching shining light from the Sun.
2. Place a mirror at the eyepiece of the binoculars.
3. Reflect the light from the Sun onto a wall opposite.
4. Adjust the image so it becomes more definite.
5. From time to time you will need to adjust the binoculars so they are in line with the Sun.

15 Sunspots

View images of the Sun safely.

Materials
- 2 pieces of cardboard
- sharp pencil

STEPS

1. Make a small hole with the sharp pencil in a piece of cardboard.
2. Go outside and stand with your back to the Sun.
3. Hold the cardboard with the hole in it up to the Sun.
4. Hold the other piece of cardboard about 8 in (20 cm) below it.
5. Observe what is happening.
6. Move the posterboard pieces farther apart.
7. Observe what is happening.

Did You Know?

Dark spots come and go all the time on the Sun's surface. These sunspots are dark because they are much cooler than the gas around them.
Warning: Never stare directly at the Sun as it will cause damage to your eyes.

16 The Moving Sun

Observe how the Sun moves through the day.

STEPS

1. Choose three times of the day to go outside and measure the Sun. The best times are mid morning, noon, and mid afternoon.
2. Before you go outside, record the three times you will be outside in a table.
3. With your partners, go outside with your chalk and your recording table.
4. Take turns to draw each other's shadows on the concrete.
5. Draw what your shadow looks like in your recording table. Draw a line through the middle of your shadow.
6. Go out for your second observation and stand in exactly the same place as you did earlier. Trace around your shadow and draw a line down the middle of it. Record this on your table.
7. Do this for your third observation.
8. Compare the lines down the middle of each shadow. What do you notice?

Materials
- chalk
- 2 friends
- pen
- paper
- watch

Did You Know?
When it is summer in the Northern Hemisphere it is winter in the Southern Hemisphere.
Warning: Never stare directly at the Sun as it will cause damage to your eyes.

You missed a bit of my shadow near my armpit, Pluto, my intergalactic friend.

17 Sunset in a Box

Why does the sky change color at sunset?

STEPS

1. Fill your box with the water.
2. Add a teaspoon of milk to the water.
3. Shine the flashlight straight down to see what the Sun looks like at midday.
4. Shine the flashlight sideways to see what the Sun looks like as it sets.

Materials
- clear plastic box
- water
- milk
- flashlight

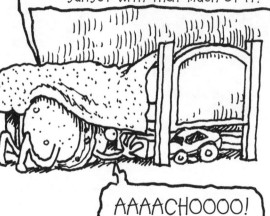

Will you look at all the dust under this bed? If you could get the setting sun under here, it would be a spectacular sunset with that much of it!

AAAACHOOOO!

Did You Know?
Earth is surrounded by an atmosphere that is full of dust particles (similar to the ones you see in a ray of sunshine shining through the window). The particles scatter light. The red and yellow light of the Sun is harder to scatter, so that is why we see those colors during a sunset.

18 Different Moons

View the different phases of the Moon.

STEPS

1. Paint the inside of a shoe box black.
2. Cut three holes, spread evenly along, on each side of the shoe box. Make the holes about ¼ in (½ cm) in diameter.
3. Cut another hole of the same size at one end of the shoe box.
4. At the other end of the shoe box cut a big enough hole for the flashlight to shine through.
5. Fix the ping pong ball in the middle of the shoe box with modeling clay or tape at the height of the holes you have cut in the sides of the shoe box.
6. Hold the flashlight in place and turn it on.
7. Look into each hole. Can you see the phases of the moon?

Materials
- shoe box
- black paint
- scissors
- modeling clay or tape
- ping pong ball
- flashlight

Did You Know?
The Moon spins exactly once during each orbit of Earth, which means we always see the same side. The other side remained a mystery until the Russian space probe Luna 3 explored it in 1956. The probe sent back pictures that showed the other side had more craters!

19 Phases of the Moon

Why does the Moon appear in different phases?

STEPS

1. Place a ball or a balloon wrapped in kitchen foil on a table.
2. Ask a friend to shine the flashlight onto one side of the Moon.
3. Turn out the lights.
4. Move to the other side of the table and observe where the light is.
5. Slowly move yourself around the table watching the Moon and its light.

My ball wrapped in kitchen foil looks just like the real Moon ... Well, sort of!

Materials
- ball or balloon wrapped in kitchen foil (the Moon)
- flashlight (the Sun)
- darkened room
- friend

Did You Know?
The Moon is our closest companion in space. It is about a quarter of the size of Earth, measuring 2,160 miles (3,475 km) across. The Moon orbits Earth about once a month and travels 1,423,000 miles (2,290,000 km). We call these phases of the Moon quarter Moon, full Moon, crescent Moon, and new Moon.

20 Moon Gazing

Observe the phases of the Moon.

Materials
- pencil
- paper
- clipboard
- clock

STEPS

1. Draw eight round moon-like shapes.

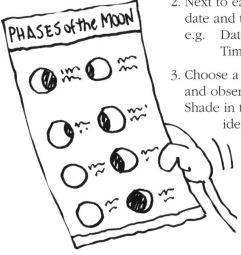

2. Next to each shape leave room for the date and time to be recorded.
   e.g. Date: Date:
   Time: Time:

3. Choose a clear night and go outside and observe the shape of the Moon. Shade in the first moon-like shape identical to the Moon in the sky.

4. Wait two nights and observe the shape of the Moon again and shade in the second circle.

5. Continue this until each of the eight moon-like shapes are completed.

Did You Know?

The Moon does not shine any of its own light onto Earth. We can see the Moon from Earth because it is reflecting the light from the Sun. On Earth it looks like the Moon is changing shape but the Moon is spinning slowly on its axis as it orbits Earth—this changes the amount of light we can see.

21 Your Weight on the Moon

Calculate what your weight would be on the Moon.

Materials
- bathroom scales
- calculator

STEPS

1. Weigh yourself on your bathroom scale.

2. Divide your weight by six because the strength of gravity on the Moon is about one-sixth of that on Earth.

Did You Know?

In 1969 Neil Armstrong and Edwin Aldrin were the first people to ever walk on the Moon. This was eight years after Yuri Gagarin made the first human space flight.

22 Reflective Telescopes

See how a reflective telescope works.

STEPS

1. Trace the area of your lamp onto the dark piece of cardboard.
2. Cut it out and then cut an arrow in the middle of the cardboard.
3. Stick the cardboard cut-out to the lamp with tape so it is blocking the light.
4. Plug the lamp into a power source and set the mirror up so that it reflects the light onto a nearby wall.
5. Hold or sit the magnifying glass (you might need to use modeling clay to keep it in place) so that the light reflecting from the mirror travels through it before hitting the wall.

Materials
- desk lamp
- dark piece of cardboard
- marker
- scissors
- tape
- small mirror
- magnifying glass
- modeling clay

I'm sure that's my cousin, Phobos. He's a moon around Mars.

Did You Know?
In a reflective telescope the light reflects off the primary mirror onto a secondary mirror, which is then focused and magnified by an eyepiece in the lens.

---

23 Refracting Telescopes

See how a refracting telescope works.

Whoa, boy! I think we're being invaded by something huge from the far-flung corners of the universe.

BUZZZ

STEPS

1. Trace the area of your lamp onto the red piece of cardboard.
2. Cut it out, and cut a star shape out from the middle of the cardboard.
3. Stick the cardboard cut-out to the lamp with tape so it is blocking the light.
4. Plug the lamp into a power source and position the lamp so it is shining onto a nearby wall.
5. Place a magnifying glass between the lamp and the wall so that the light passes through it. You might need modeling clay to keep the magnifying glass in its place. Observe the image on the wall.
6. Place the second magnifying glass behind the first; again, you might need modeling clay. Gently move the second magnifying glass until the star image appears on the wall.

Materials
- desk lamp
- red cardboard
- marker
- scissors
- tape
- 2 magnifying glasses
- modeling clay

Did You Know?
Our brains work out how big an object is by using the angle of the light as it enters our eyes. A telescope makes distant objects appear larger by bending this light. The light rays from a distant object change direction as they move through the lens and again as they leave. The eyepiece or the lens brings the image into focus.

24 Stars in the Day

Can you see stars in the daytime?

STEPS

1. Use your hole punch to make holes in the cardboard. These holes will represent stars.
2. Put the piece of cardboard inside a white envelope.
3. Turn the lights off in a room and shine a lamp onto the front of the envelope. The envelope reflects the light so you cannot see the stars inside.
4. Try shining the light from behind the envelope.

Materials
- paper
- hole punch
- cardboard
- white envelope
- lamp

That makes me homesick!

Did You Know?
You can see the stars better in the country than in the city. In the city, pollution and streetlights make it more difficult to see faint lights in the sky.

---

25 Gazing at Stars

Galaxies are moving away from each other. How does this happen?

STEPS

1. Blow up your balloon to half its capacity but do not tie it.
2. With your marker draw small specks all over the balloon.
3. Blow more air into the balloon and then note the position of the specks.
4. Keep blowing and observing the specks. What do you notice?

Materials
- balloon
- waterproof marker

A few more puffs and my balloon will be the size of the Universe... well, sort of.

Did You Know?
Scientists think that the Universe is growing in size just like your balloon did. This means that the galaxies are moving away from each other, leaving more and more distance between them.

26 Star Motion

Become familiar with the movement of stars.

STEPS

1. Trace your star map onto a piece of paper and push a pin through all the points of the paper that have a star.
2. Ask someone to hold your paper and shine a flashlight from the bottom so that the holes made by the pins are seen on your ceiling.
3. Use your adhesive putty to stick a small piece of paper where each pin prick appears on the ceiling.
4. Use your map to help you locate Polaris (the Pole star) and the Big Dipper. You can ask an adult to help you.
5. When you have located Polaris, stand directly underneath it and slowly turn yourself in an counterclockwise direction.

That pinhole is Polaris ... that pinhole is The Big Dipper ... that pinhole ... is just a pinhole.

Materials
- flashlight
- adhesive putty
- small, round piece of paper (from a hole punch)
- paper
- star map
- pins

Did You Know?
What you have just observed is how the stars would appear to move at the North Pole because Polaris is almost directly above the North Pole.

27 Black Holes

Simulate what astronomers see when a black hole moves in front of a distant object.

STEPS

1. Hold your magnifying glass just above the newspaper print.
2. Move it back and forth slowly.
3. What you see is what astronomers see.

Beware of the Black Hole! I saw half of the Universe disappear into one of these once!

Materials
- magnifying glass
- newspaper

Did You Know?
Because black holes suck in light, astronomers can't see them. They have to look for gravity swirling around the hole just as water does around a bathtub drain.

28 Star Gazing

Observe the movement of stars.

Materials
- pencil
- paper
- clipboard

STEPS

1. Wait until it is dark. Find a place away from street and house lights that has a good view of the stars.
2. Record the exact spot that you are standing on so you can return to it later.
3. Observe the night sky.
4. Choose a star that is bright or easily located (near a tree top or roof).
5. Sketch the star, and if you can, any surrounding stars.
6. Use your finger, hand or arm to measure and describe distances between stars and objects.
7. You can record your findings in words and illustrations. Remember to also record the time.
8. Wait half an hour and repeat steps 5 to 7.
9. Wait another half an hour and repeat again.
10. You can continue this until bedtime!

Note: As an extension to this experiment, you could plan a trip to a local observatory. On a clear night you can do some real star and planet gazing that will amaze you.

Did You Know?

Earth is like a grain of sand on the beach of the Universe! Our Sun is just one of billions in the Universe. There are about 100,000 million stars in the Milky Way. The nearest star to our Sun is so far away that its light takes about four years to reach Earth. To travel across our galaxy would take about 100,000 years. There are an estimated 100,000 million galaxies—and that is just what we can see with our largest telescopes!

29 Splitting Light

Light is composed of different colors. See how a spectroscope splits the light from stars and planets.

Materials
- thick cardboard
- straight drinking glass
- water
- paper

STEPS

1. Make a long, narrow cut from the bottom of the cardboard to just above the height of the glass.
2. Sit the glass on the piece of paper in front of a window that lets in a lot of sun and place the cardboard between the glass and the window (remember to have the cut in the cardboard running the length of the glass).
3. You should see the light split into colors.

Did You Know?

Spectroscopes have allowed astronomers to study what the Universe is actually made of. Astronomers who study this are called astrophysicists.

30 Making a Spiral Galaxy

Make a spiral galaxy.

STEPS

1. Put the coin under the dish so that you can spin it easily.
2. Pour about ½ in (1 cm) of water into the dish.
3. Gently sprinkle your paper in the middle of the dish.
4. Slowly spin the dish and watch what happens to the paper in the middle.

Did You Know?

Galaxies live together in clusters just like cows live in a herd. Sometimes they bump into each other and disturb each other's shape. When this happens, it can cause new stars to be born and this can create an amazing display of fireworks.

Materials

- shallow dish
- coin
- water
- small circles of paper (confetti)

31 Speeding Stars

See how outer and inner stars of spiral galaxies travel at different speeds.

STEPS

1. Half fill a glass with water.
2. Place the paper strip inside the top section of the glass so it is lying over the water.
3. Gently add the methylated spirits.
4. Very carefully remove the paper.
5. Slowly add the oil and examine what happens.
6. Turn the glass sharply.
7. Leave for about 30 seconds and examine what has happened.

Materials

- drinking glass
- paper strip about 8 in (20 cm) long × 2 in (5 cm) wide
- cooking oil
- methylated spirit
- teaspoon
- water

That's where I grew up, between those two galaxies. Those stars were right across the street from us.

Did You Know?

In the Southern Hemisphere, if you can find a clear night away from city lights, you may be able to view the galaxies of the two Magellan clouds and Andromeda.

32 Space Clouds

See how a dust cloud would block an astronomer's view of space.

Materials
- white balloon
- light or lamp
- tissue paper

STEPS
1. Turn on a light or lamp.
2. Think about the color of the light.
3. Blow up a balloon, hold it up to your face, and look at the light.
4. Slowly let some of the air out of the balloon and look at the light again.
5. Look at the light through one sheet of tissue paper.
6. Try two pieces, then three.

I feel just like an astronomer who can't see the Universe for dust.

Did You Know?
Dust and gas are a part of the galaxy. Coalsack is a cloud that is situated between the Southern Cross and the nearer Pointer. It blocks the light of stars behind it and prevents astronomers from seeing beyond it.

33 Your Own Quadrant

Make your own quadrant that can help you map the night sky.

Materials
- cardboard
- scissors
- protractor
- ruler
- pen or pencil
- string
- modeling clay

STEPS
1. Cut the cardboard into the shape of a quarter of a circle.
2. Mark out the degrees onto the curved edge of the cardboard with a protractor and ruler.
3. Cut a piece of string a little longer than the cardboard.
4. Attach a ball of modeling clay to the end of the string and tie the other end to the right angle of the quarter circle.
5. Cut two identical squares about 1¼ in (3 cm) apart to be your viewfinder.
6. Attach them to the upper side of your quadrant.
7. Point your quadrant to the sky and line up a star by the viewfinder. The string will dangle at the degrees of the star to the horizon.

Did You Know?
Before astronomers had telescopes, they could only use quadrants to map objects in the sky. Quadrants tell an astronomer a star's elevation from the horizon. One of the first astronomers was an Italian named Galileo who, in 1609, turned his telescope upward into the night sky and saw, among many things, more details of the Moon.

34 Star Gazers

Stars are born, live for a long time, and die.

STEPS

1. Cut out a giant star from your cardboard and paint it silver. You can decorate it with sequins and glitter.
2. Draw two circles, one on the black paper and one on the white. Cut them out.
3. Divide the black circle into six equal parts. In each part use your pastels to draw the life cycle of a star (you may use a book to help).
4. Glue the black circle to the star.
5. Paint the other white circle to match your star, but cut out a part of it big enough to show one of the parts of your black circle.
6. Attach the new circle to the black one with a paper fastener.
7. Turn the disk around.

Whoops! There goes another star.

Materials
- cardboard
- black and white paper
- scissors
- glue
- paper fasteners
- glitter
- sequins
- silver paint
- pastels
- ruler
- pencil

Did You Know?
When a star dies it self-destructs and causes an explosion brighter than a million Suns!

---

35 Bedroom Nights

Make your very own night sky in your bedroom.

STEPS

1. Take the large piece of black cardboard or paper.
2. Use your glue to create night sky patterns.
3. Sprinkle your glitter over the glue.
4. Cut out stars from the metallic paper to stick on your paper.
5. Use the silver thread to outline your stars.
6. Stick the cardboard or paper on your bedroom ceiling. (Ask a parent first.)
7. Before you go to bed, shine your flashlight on your ceiling to see the sky.

Twenty-two thousand six hundred and seven. Twenty-two thousand six hundred and eight ... boy! It's going to take a while to count all the stars in the sky!

Materials
- black cardboard or paper (large piece)
- glitter
- glue
- metallic paints
- silver thread
- shiny metallic paper
- flashlight
- scissors

Did You Know?
On a nice, clear night you should be able to see thousands of stars twinkling in the night sky.

36 How Old Are You Really?

Would your age be different on other planets?

STEPS

1. The first thing you need to do is put your own age into the calculator.
2. Now you need to press divide on the calculator and then press in the planet's period of revolution around the Sun. (For example, if you want to work out how old you would be on Mars you would press 12 ÷ 1.88 = 6.38 years old!)
3. Now you know how old you would be if you lived on another planet! Alternatively, you don't have to use a calculator, you could try working it out by yourself!

Materials
- paper
- pen
- calculator

Planet	Period of revolution (compared to Earth)
Mercury	0.241 Earth years (87.9 Earth days)
Venus	0.615 Earth years (224.7 Earth days)
Earth	1.0 Earth year (365 Earth days)
Mars	1.88 Earth years (686.9 Earth days)
Jupiter	11.9 Earth years (4,343.5 Earth days)
Saturn	29.5 Earth years (10,767.5 Earth days)
Uranus	84.0 Earth years (30,660 Earth days)
Neptune	164.8 Earth years (60,152 Earth days)
Pluto*	248.5 Earth years (90,702.5 Earth days)

Did You Know?

There are eight planets in our solar system and Saturn is the second biggest planet, but did you know it is also the lightest planet? It is also the only planet in our solar system that could float in water.

*Dwarf planet

37 Potato Asteroids

Make and bake some "asteroids."

Materials
- baking sheet
- potato
- oven
- oven mitts
- mixing bowl and large spoon
- 4 to 8 cups of mashed potatoes
- ¼ cup (½ stick) of butter or margarine
- pan
- potato masher

STEPS

1. Turn on your oven to 375°F (190°C). Ask an adult to help.
2. Take a little slice of the butter or margarine and rub it evenly on the baking sheet.
3. Make the mashed potatoes (a lot—eight cups, or a little—four cups).
4. Add butter or margarine, salt and pepper to the potatoes and mix well. The mixture should stick together. If it's too dry, add a little milk.
5. Take a handful of mashed potato (about ½ cup or more) and shape it into your own idea of an interesting asteroid shape. Use your fingers to poke dents in it for craters.
6. Set the asteroid on the greased baking sheet.
7. Put the baking sheet full of asteroids in the hot oven for about 20 to 25 minutes, or until they are brown.
8. Using the oven mitts remove the baking sheet from the oven, and using the large spoon transfer the asteroids to a serving plate.
9. Enjoy your asteroids.

I'm not really an asteroid. I'm just a potato on a baking sheet. But don't tell anybody!

Did You Know?

Asteroids are chunks of rock that never quite made it to fully-fledged planethood when our solar system formed. Most of them orbit the Sun in a "belt" between Mars (the fourth planet) and Jupiter (the fifth planet). But some asteroids have orbits that cross or come close to Earth's orbit.

---

38 Greenhouse Effect

Create the greenhouse effect as it would be on Venus.

Materials
- outdoor thermometer
- glass jar with a lid
- sunlight

STEPS

1. Put the jar outside in the sun with the lid off and place the thermometer inside with the bulb facing the bottom of the jar.
2. Wait for a couple of minutes for the temperature to stabilize and then record the temperature.
3. Put the thermometer inside the jar with the bulb facing the sky. Put the lid on and place it in the sun with the lid facing down.
4. Wait for the temperature to stop moving and then record it.

That Sun sure is hot. I'm glad I don't live on Venus.

Did You Know?

Strong rays of light hit the surface of Venus and heat it up, but the clouds and carbon dioxide in the atmosphere do not allow the heat to escape. This means that Venus never cools down because the hot air is trapped there.

39 Orbiting the Sun

See how the planets orbit around the Sun.

Materials
- piece of paper
- two pins
- pencil
- string

Did You Know?

At the heart of our solar system is a star, the Sun. Nine planets move around the Sun in elliptical paths or orbits. Pluto is the farthest known planet from the Sun, and was recently classified as a dwarf planet. At certain times, Pluto's orbit actually moves in front of Neptune, making Neptune the farthest planet at that time.

Each time a planet orbits the Sun once, it has traveled one year. Each time you celebrate a birthday Earth has completed another orbit of the Sun.

STEPS

1. On opposite sides of a piece of paper insert two pins.
2. Loosely fit a piece of string around the two pins.
3. Tie the string.
4. Pretend your pencil is a planet and place it on the inside of the string and move it in a circle around the pins so it tightens the string.

---

40 Rusty Mars

Re-create the rusty color of the planet Mars.

Materials
- a key (not stainless steel or galvanized)

STEPS

1. Take a new key and leave it outside.
2. Make sure the area is damp.
3. Collect the key in a couple of weeks.
4. See the pinkish-brown color of the rusty key.

Did You Know?

Mars is smaller than Earth and it gets less warmth from the Sun. Its average temperature is just −131°F (−90°C). If you look at Mars in a clear sky at night you can see its pinkish color.

41 Our Solar System

Create a mobile that represents stars and planets.

STEPS

1. Tear the newspaper into pieces and leave them overnight to soak in a bucket of water.
2. Squeeze the water out of the newspaper.
3. Make the round shapes of the planets by dipping the paper into the paste and molding them into different sized balls.
4. Leave the shapes out to dry.
5. Paint the balls so that they are the different colors of the planets.
6. Make stars with your wire to hang next to your planets.
7. Push the needle through each ball, and thread the wire through the hole.
8. Attach your wire to the two bamboo sticks which have been made into a cross shape.
9. Turn the lights off and shine a flashlight onto the mobile.

Materials
- newspaper
- bucket
- glue
- paints
- bamboo sticks
- thread
- wire
- needle
- flashlight

Did You Know?
Our solar system was formed more than four billion years ago.

---

42 Uranus and the Sun

What does the planet Uranus look like when it is orbiting the Sun?

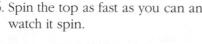

STEPS

1. Draw two circles and cut them out.
2. Make a cut from the outside of the circle to the middle and make a cone shape. Leave a small hole at the top.
3. Poke a stick through the cones to join them together so that they look like a spinning top.
4. Paint and decorate the top half of the top with warm colors like reds and gold.
5. Paint and decorate the bottom half of the top with cold colors like blues and greens.
6. Spin the top as fast as you can and watch it spin.

Materials
- stick
- glue
- paints
- cardboard
- pencils
- scissors
- glitter

Did You Know?
Uranus looks like it is lying on its side when it goes around the Sun. This means that one side of the planet is in darkness and away from light, while the other side is in the line of the Sun and is warmer.

43 E.T. Rocks

See if you can collect some extra-terrestrial rocks.

Materials
- white paper (large piece)
- magnet
- magnifying glass

STEPS

1. Go outside on a sunny day and secure your large piece of paper to an area that is not under cover.
2. Leave the paper there for 4–6 hours. (Do not leave it out in the rain.)
3. Collect the paper gently. Make sure you gather it so that anything you have collected rolls into the middle of the paper.
4. Hold your magnet under the paper and lightly shake off the material gathered. The material not attracted to your magnet will just fall off.
5. Collect the material that did not fall off and look at it through a magnifying glass.
6. Extra-terrestrial rocks are usually dark round particles with pitted surfaces.

Did You Know?
Every day tons of particles fall to Earth from meteorites. You will not feel them, or see them, unless you look very carefully because they are miniscule.

44 Meteorites & Craters

The size, angle, and speed of a meteorite's impact affects the properties of its crater.

Materials
- 2 shallow basins (cat litter boxes work well)
- ruler
- 2 bags of flour
- pencil
- box of instant cocoa
- newspaper
- several pebbles, various sizes
- chair

STEPS

1. Fill one of the basins with flour about 1–1½ in (2½–4 cm) deep. Spread the newspaper out and place the basin on top.
2. Sprinkle a little cocoa on the surface.
3. Pick out one of the smallest pebbles, stand on a chair, and drop (not throw) the pebble into the basin.
4. Observe and try to predict the appearance of a crater formed by a larger pebble dropped from the same height.
5. Repeat step 3, but this time with a medium-sized pebble. What is different?
6. Repeat step 3, again, but this time with the largest pebble.
7. Repeat steps 3 to 5 but this time vary the height. Smooth the flour and sprinkle on more cocoa. Try again, varying the force, size, and angle of your "meteorite."

Did You Know?
All craters that we have seen on the Moon and Earth are pretty much circular. The reason is that an explosion occurs on impact and the forces associated with an explosion are always spherically symmetrical.

45 Meteor Burnout

See how a meteor burns up as it enters Earth's atmosphere.

STEPS

1. Fill up the plastic bottle with water.
2. Drop the tablet into the water.
3. Observe.

Materials
- plastic bottle
- water
- ½ antacid tablet

Did You Know?

Meteors are small rock-like chunks that are probably broken pieces of comets or asteroids that travel around in outer space. They burn up as they enter and pass through Earth's atmosphere.

46 Rocket Launch

Experience a rocket launch.

STEPS

1. Rockets have fins to help them fly. Cut out four 8 in (20 cm) long fin shaped pieces of cardboard, as per diagram.
2. Fold over the flap of the fin and with tape attach it to the bottle.
3. Use the funnel to half fill the bottle with water.
4. Use the corkscrew to carefully drill a hole through the cork.
5. Push the wide end of the valve into the tubing.
6. Push the valve through the hole in the cork.
7. Push the cork and the valve into the top of the plastic bottle. Make sure it fits firmly.
8. Attach the other end of the plastic tubing to the bicycle pump.
9. Turn your rocket the right way up—so that the cork is on the ground.
10. Pump the bicycle pump.

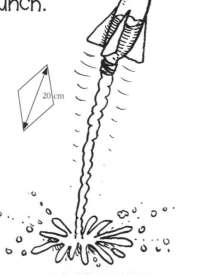

Materials
- cardboard
- pen
- ruler
- scissors
- plastic bottle
- tape
- funnel
- jug of water
- cork
- corkscrew
- air valve
- plastic tubing
- bicycle pump

Did You Know?

The force of a rocket comes from the amount of propellant it shoots out. The water in the bottle is the propellant. Compressed air above the water provides the energy that makes the thrust.

Warning: Launch your rocket in an open space away from buildings and trees.

47 Rocork Launch!

Launch a mini rocket.

Did You Know?

A chemical reaction between the vinegar (representing liquid oxygen) and the baking soda (representing fuel) produces carbon dioxide gas. The pressure inside the bottle pushes against the cork. In real rockets the gas is jetted out of the actual spacecraft, propelling it forward! **Warning**: When the rocork is about to launch make sure you are a safe distance away.

"You don't really think they use vinegar and baking soda in our engines do you?"

"I don't know. But if they do it works pretty well."

Materials
- teaspoon of baking soda
- paper towel about 4 in × 8 in (10 cm × 20 cm)
- ½ cup of water
- ½ cup of vinegar
- paper streamers or ribbons
- thumb tack
- plastic bottle
- cork that fits the bottle

STEPS

1. Place the baking soda on the middle of the paper towel.
2. Roll up the towel and twist the ends to keep the baking soda inside.
3. Pour the water and vinegar into the bottle.
4. Cut out some streamers or ribbons and with a thumb tack attach them to the cork.
5. Drop the paper towel into the bottle and very quickly push the cork into the bottle.
6. Place the bottle in an outside area that is away from windows etc.
7. Stand well away and watch.

48 Balloon Rocket

... 3, 2, 1, lift off!

STEPS

1. Carefully cut out the bottoms of two paper or plastic cups and sit one of the cups inside the other.
2. Partly blow up the long balloon. Hold closed but do not tie.
3. Slide the drinking cups over the untied end of the balloon.
4. Fold the untied end of the balloon over the side of the cup and tape it down firmly so air cannot escape.
5. Place the round balloon inside the cups and blow up the balloon.
6. Hold the end of the round balloon closed but do not tie.
7. Hold the rocket so it is facing the sky.
8. Unstick the long balloon's end.
9. Let go of the round balloon.

Materials
- 2 paper or plastic drinking cups
- scissors
- tape
- long balloon
- round balloon

Did You Know?

Rockets transport people to the Moon. We live on the Earth. The Moon is the only place in our solar system that people have visited.

49 Bubble Rocket

Build a bubble-powered rocket.

STEPS

1. Cut your paper to make a rocket shape.

2. Insert the film canister inside the rocket and attach it with tape. Make sure the lid of the canister is facing down.

3. Cut out a circle shape. Roll it into a cone and attach it to the top of your rocket.

4. Put on your sunglasses.

5. Turn the rocket upside down and take off the film canister lid.

6. Fill the canister one-third full of water and drop the tablet in (you must do these steps quickly).

7. Put the lid back on and place your rocket the right way up on your driveway or any piece of concrete.

8. Stand back and watch it blast off.

Materials
- paper
- photo film canister
- tape
- scissors
- antacid tablet
- paper towels
- water
- sunglasses

Did You Know?

A real rocket works the same way that yours does, but instead of using an antacid tablet, it uses rocket fuel. The antacid tablet releases bubbles and when the air escapes from the bubbles it pushes the sides of the canister. The canister cannot expand so it pops its lid and the rocket takes off!

---

50 Centrifugal Force

What is centrifugal force?

STEPS

1. Tie the string to the top of the carrot with the leaves.

2. Slip the other end of the string through the large spool and then attach it to the small spool by tying it up.

3. Hold the large spool and begin making circles with your hand. The small spool should lift in the air.

4. Watch the carrot to see what happens.

Materials
- string
- carrot with the leaves still attached
- large spool
- small spool

Did You Know?

The force of the rotation acts as a pulling force. This pulling force is what causes the carrot to move. Centrifugal force is the force that pulls away from the center circle.

51 Working in Space

How do astronauts feel when they are working in space?

Materials
- nuts and bolts
- rubber gloves
- big bowl
- water

STEPS

1. Place the nuts and bolts onto a table and try picking them up and screwing them together.
2. Put on a pair of rubber gloves (these represent spacesuit gloves) and try to do the same thing.
3. Fill the bowl with water.
4. Add the nuts and bolts.
5. Try to pick up the nuts and bolts and screw them together under the water.

Wearing these heavy rubber astronaut gloves (Mom's dishwashing gloves) to screw this nut and bolt together makes me feel just like a real astronaut.

Did You Know?

Bulky spacesuits make it very hard for astronauts to work in space. Heavy and stiff spacesuits tire out astronauts quickly and prevent them from feeling things properly.

---

52 Robot Arms

Become an astronaut and work a robot arm.

Materials
- thick cardboard
- scissors
- ruler
- corkscrew
- 2 cotter (split) pins
- dowel
- picture hook
- 2 paper clips
- modeling clay

Oh my! That looks like a job for the robotic arm.

STEPS

1. Measure out three cardboard strips about 12 in (30 cm) × 2 in (5 cm).
2. Cut them out.
3. Use the corkscrew to make a hole about ¾ in (2 cm) from both ends of each strip.
4. Join the strips with cotter (split) pins.
5. Bend one of the paper clips into an "s" shape and slide it through the hole at the end of the arm.
6. Take the hook and screw it into the end of the dowel.
7. Pass the hook on the dowel through the hole in the end of the cardboard. Move the doweling to move the robot arm.
8. Make a ball out of the modeling clay and gently push in the second paper clip.
9. Try to pick up the modeling clay ball with the robot arm.

Did You Know?

If satellites break down, astronauts need to fix them. Robot arms are used by astronauts to rebuild and fix these satellites.

53 Aliens in the Night

Do aliens exist? Play a game with shadows.

STEPS

1. Draw an imaginary alien shape on the cardboard.
2. Cut out the alien figure.
3. Make up as many alien characters as you like.
4. Bend the straw and stick the shorter end to the back of the alien.
5. Push one straw into the other to make a longer handle.
6. Place two chairs about 3 ft (1 m) apart.
7. Tie string between the two chairs.
8. Pin the sheet onto the string as the curtain.
9. Place the flashlight or lamp behind the curtain and the puppet.
10. Perform a play about aliens.

Materials
- colored pens/pencils
- white sheet
- scissors
- string
- cardboard
- clothespins
- tape
- chairs
- bendy straws
- flashlight or lamp

Did You Know?

So far the only place in the Universe known to have life is Earth. Many astronomers believe that life might exist elsewhere in the Universe.

54 Shadow Dances

Make a shadow dance.

STEPS

1. Cut a small strip from the Styrofoam and push the toothpick into it. Put this strip onto the piece of cardboard.
2. Shine your flashlight on the toothpick to make a shadow.
3. Move the flashlight to change what the shadow looks like. Do not move the toothpick. How have you changed it and what did you do?
4. Now move the toothpick but do not move the flashlight. What happens to your shadow now?
5. You can move your shadow using just the sun and the toothpick.
6. Note any changes in the shadow when you use the flashlight and the sunlight.

Materials
- glue or tape
- cardboard
- Styrofoam
- toothpick
- flashlight

AHHRR! What a horrible alien. I can't bear to look...

Did You Know?

The differences in the light sources happen because the Sun is farther away and therefore the angles of the shadow may not have been noticeably different.

55 Travel to the Moon

How hard is it to reach a moving target?

STEPS

1. Measure and cut a piece of string about 24 in (60 cm) long.
2. Stick one end of the string to the ruler.
3. Tie a washer to the other end of the string.
4. Place the ruler on the edge of a table so that the string is hanging over.
5. Keep the ruler in place by putting a heavy book on top.
6. Try to hit the washer with the paper balls.
7. Swing the washer and try to hit it with the paper balls.

Materials
- string
- ruler
- scissors
- tape
- metal washer
- books
- small pieces of paper scrunched into balls

Did You Know?

Plotting a course through space is not easy—both the spacecraft and the Moon or planet are moving. To save fuel, rockets are aimed at where the Moon or planet will be when the rocket is ready to land.

---

56 Eating in Space

What do astronauts eat in space?

STEPS

1. Puree the vegetables.
2. Place pureed vegetables or baby food into a plastic bag.
3. Freeze.
4. Place the plastic bag into the microwave and heat.
5. Eat!

Materials
- baby food or pureed vegetables
- microwave oven
- plastic bag

Did You Know?

Space crews eat three meals a day. They can choose from about 70 menus. These meals are planned before the mission begins.

57 Astronaut Suits

How does it feel to be in a spacesuit?

STEPS

1. Put on both pairs of coveralls.
2. Stuff scrunched up newspaper in between the two coveralls.
3. Put on the ski gloves, ski boots, and helmet.
4. Place some books into a backpack and put the backpack onto your back.
5. Slowly walk around the house. Take note of how you feel and move.
6. Now try to pick up items in your house, such as books or a drinking glass.

I must keep my lifeline attached. I don't want to float away ... out of the family room.

Materials
- 2 large pairs of coveralls
- newspaper
- ski gloves
- ski boots or rubber boots
- motorcycle or bicycle helmet
- backpack
- books

Did You Know?

Spacesuits protect the astronauts from the airless vacuum of space. Without the suits the astronauts' blood would boil and they would die within seconds. Spacesuits are like having an individual spacecraft, giving astronauts help with cooling, oxygen, and power.

---

58 Super Hearing

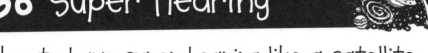

How to have super hearing like a satellite.

STEPS

1. Roll the cardboard into a cone shape but make sure you leave a small hole at the pointy end. Leave the large hole as big as you can.
2. Put tape on the cone to hold it in place.
3. Place the small end of the cone near your ear and go outside.
4. Take note of the sounds you hear. Are noises louder or softer?

This cone works just like a satellite dish. I can hear things from far, far away. I think Mom's calling me for dinner.

Materials
- cardboard (large piece)
- clear tape

Did You Know?

A satellite dish has a cone shape stuck to its surface. The small end points to the sky and the large end is stuck to the dish. This means that people in space can send messages to the satellite dish because they have the small end of the cone.

59 Flying in Space

You can create a gliding machine.

STEPS

1. Cut a little hole in the middle of the lid.

2. Put the squirt top over the hole and glue it to the lid making sure that no air can escape from the hole. Make sure the writing on top of the lid is facing up.

3. Blow up the balloon and slip the opening over the squirt top. Make sure the squirt top is closed.

4. Place the lid on a smooth table and lift the squirt top opening and see what happens.

Materials
- scissors
- plastic lid from a container, e.g. a margarine tub
- squirt top from a dishwashing liquid bottle
- glue
- balloon

Did You Know?
An air cushion is created when you let the balloon's air out of the squirt top. It is this air cushion that allows your glider to lift up.

---

60 Signals and Satellites

Satellites sent into space redirect signals and information.

STEPS

1. Cut out a piece of cardboard that is big enough to cover the can.

2. Stick the cardboard onto the can and stand the can upright.

3. Cut a 4 in (10 cm) square out of the piece of cardboard and stick it to the can so that it appears to one side (this will act as the antenna of the satellite).

4. Place the aluminum can onto the floor and measure approximately 3 ft (1 m).

5. Position the mirror at the end of the yard measured.

6. Place the flashlight so it is level with the aluminum can but sitting about 8 in (20 cm) away.

7. Turn the lights off in the room and close the curtains.

8. Turn on the flashlight. Adjust the mirror so that it reflects the light from the flashlight onto the dark card on the side of the can (the antenna).

Materials
- dark cardboard
- scissors
- aluminum can
- tape
- measuring tape
- mirror
- flashlight
- modeling clay

Did You Know?
Communication satellites enable radio transmissions to be sent anywhere on Earth! Radio signals are transmitted from one side of the planet and are aimed at an orbiting satellite. The satellite then redirects this information to a receiver on the opposite side of the world!

61 Orbiting Satellites

See how a satellite orbits (travels) around Earth and relays information.

Materials
- friend
- string or yarn (two different colors)
- colored tape (two different colors)

STEPS

1. Use one of the colored tapes to make a circle about 20 in (50 cm) in diameter (representing Earth).
2. Stand inside the circle and take three very big steps.
3. Use the other colored tape to make a circle at this spot (the orbit of the satellite).
4. Cut a piece of yarn from both colors about 4 in (10 cm) bigger than the distance from the two circles.
5. Stand on the smaller circle and hold a piece of yarn in each hand (to represent the transmitter and receiver).
6. Ask your friend to stand on the outer circle and hold both pieces of yarn in one hand.
7. Both you and your friend slowly turn around by walking along the taped circle.

Did You Know?

The movement, or the orbit, of a satellite around Earth is fixed. The satellite follows this orbit until it is no longer needed in space. There are about 2,500 satellites that have been sent into space orbiting around Earth.

62 Finding Your Bearings

How to find your bearings in space.

Materials
- map (of where you are)
- compass
- protractor
- ruler
- pencil

STEPS

1. Look at an object that you can see on your map.
2. Point your compass north and read off the angle that points toward your object.
3. This is the object bearing from where you are standing.
4. Now on the map draw a line that runs through the object at the same angle to north as the bearing you took (the top of the map is usually north).
5. Repeat this for a different object.
6. Where the two lines cross on the map is your location.

Did You Know?

Global Positioning System (GPS) satellites orbit the Earth every 12 hours.

BIOLOGY

BIOLOGY: THE STUDY OF LIVING ORGANISMS;
THE PLANTS AND ANIMALS OF A PARTICULAR AREA.

Date:	Experiment:	Notes:

63 Classifying Living Things

Classify living things into groups.

Materials
- old magazines
- scissors

STEPS

1. Cut out all the pictures of animals you can find in the magazines.
2. Decide how you are going to sort and classify these animals. You can choose to sort them by the number of legs they have; where they live; what country they are from; whether they are carnivores or herbivores; whether they are fast or slow, land or sea animals; whether they are active in the day time or the night time; and so on. There are hundreds of ways you could sort these animals.
3. Play this game with a friend. Sort them and ask your friend to guess how you classified the animals. Switch roles. See if you can trick your friend with something like marsupial or monotreme.
4. You can play this game with plants and bugs too.

What's small, green, slimy, has four legs, hops and lives in swamps, my green, slimy, hoppy little friend?

Us!

WHY?

Animals can be classified into six groups. Mammals are warm-blooded and most give birth to live young. Birds are warm-blooded and have feathers and lay eggs. Reptiles are cold-blooded and lay eggs. Amphibians are cold-blooded and can live in water and on land. Fish are cold-blooded and use gills to breathe because they live in water. Invertebrates are animals that do not have backbones.

Did You Know?

Every animal is unique in some way, just like people. And just like people, there are some things the same, such as their likes and dislikes and the number of legs they have.

64 Withered Potatoes

Make a potato shrink and shrivel.

Materials
- 1 potato
- 2 saucers
- chopping board
- knife
- salt
- water

STEPS

1. Cut the potato in half.
2. Fill both saucers with water. Mix some salt into one saucer. Leave the other one with just plain water. Mark the one with salt water so you remember which one it is.
3. Place one half of the potato into each saucer, with the flat side facing down. Leave for about half an hour. What has happened after this time?

I need to drink more water after my run around the pool. I feel like a withered potato.

Anyone got a cup of pond water?

Did You Know?

The salt water draws the water out of the potato, causing it to shrivel and become dehydrated. Dehydrated means when the water is removed. This often happens to humans when they sweat a lot and don't drink enough water. Your body can be like the potato if you don't drink enough water to replace what you sweat out!

---

65 Growing Both Ends

Grow roots and leaves from a potato.

Materials
- 1 sweet potato
- toothpicks
- drinking glass
- water

STEPS

1. Fill the drinking glass with water.
2. Stick some toothpicks in the middle of the potato so that they poke out.
3. Place the potato into the drinking glass. The toothpicks will stop the potato touching the bottom of the glass. Make sure the bottom part of the potato is touching the water.
4. Leave it for a few days. The bottom part of the potato will sprout roots and leaves will grow out of the top.

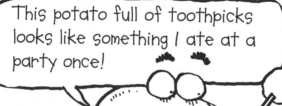

This potato full of toothpicks looks like something I ate at a party once!

Did You Know?

Potatoes are known as a root vegetable. This means that they grow from the roots of the plants under the ground. Do you know any other root vegetables? Carrots are another one.

66 Breathing Plants

How do plants obtain nutrients from the soil?

Materials
- plastic bottle
- flower with stem attached
- water
- small amount of modeling clay
- drinking straw

STEPS

1. Fill the bottle three-quarters full with water.
2. Wrap the clay around the stem of the flower.
3. Place the flower in the bottle. Use the clay to seal and close the mouth of the bottle tightly.
4. Carefully push the straw through the clay. Do not let the straw touch the water. Make sure the clay is still sealed tightly around the straw and there are no leaks.
5. Check that the straw is not touching the water. Stand in front of a mirror and suck on the straw.

I'd prefer sarsaparilla ... but for the sake of the experiment I'll give this a try. And not a bad looking toad, I might add!

Did You Know?

Plants are like straws. In their leaves are tiny little pores or holes, so tiny that you cannot see them without magnification. These pores are used by plants to breathe air. When you are sucking on the straw and removing the air from the bottle, the pores in the plant are breathing air into the bottle. Pretty clever!

67 Slippery Leaves

See if leaves lose their moisture.

Materials
- 4 fresh large leaves with a small part of the stem still attached
- string
- scissors
- ruler or stick
- petroleum jelly

STEPS

1. Tie a piece of string to the stem on each leaf. Then tie the other end of the string to the stick or ruler. Spread the leaves out so that they are not touching each other.
2. On the first leaf smear petroleum jelly on both sides. On the second leaf put petroleum jelly only on the bottom side of the leaf and on the third only on the top side of the leaf. Leave the last leaf without any petroleum jelly.
3. Leave for a few days and note the differences.

Did You Know?

The leaf with no petroleum jelly will shrivel and die first. This is because the water from the leaf has "evaporated" into the air. The petroleum jelly stops the water evaporating from the leaf pores as quickly. This is why the leaf with petroleum jelly on both sides stays fresh for the longest time.

68 Mini Greenhouse

Make a mini greenhouse to grow plants.

STEPS

1. Wash the bottle carefully so that it is clean. Don't worry if it is still wet inside.
2. Cut the bottle in half.
3. Take the bottom part of the bottle and half fill it with soil.
4. Plant the seedling in the soil, making sure you cover all the roots.
5. Place the top half of the bottle back onto the bottom half and use the tape to seal them together, making sure there are no leaks.
6. Put a few drops of water into the bottle. Place the cap back on.
7. Leave your mini greenhouse near a window where it will get plenty of sun.
8. After a few days you will notice the bottle "sweating". If it is too moist open it up and let it dry out for a while.

Materials
- clear plastic bottle
- soil
- small plant or seedling
- wide tape
- scissors

Well it looks as hot as a tropical swamp inside this bottle ... but this little plant sure loves it!

Did You Know?
The sun causes the temperature inside the greenhouse to rise. Because the lid is sealed the air inside stays heated, even when air outside the greenhouse cools down. This means the air inside turns to water that feeds the plant to keep it alive.

---

69 Sweating Plants

Water vapor is given off by plants.

STEPS

1. Water the potted plant first, making sure you fill the plant to the bottom so that the roots are well watered.
2. Cover the plant and the pot with the plastic bag. Secure the bag to the pot with the rubber band so that no air can escape.
3. Leave the plant overnight. The next day you will notice water in the bag.

Materials
- potted plant
- clear plastic bag
- water
- jug
- large rubber band

It's so hot in here! I feel like a daisy that's run laps around the flower bed then been stuck in a plastic bag.

Did You Know?
The moisture inside the bag is not sweat but water. This comes from the plant drawing in the water from the soil and giving off water vapor from its leaves. This is turned into water and stays on the inside of the bag.

70 Magic Balloon

Use gas made from yeast to blow up a balloon.

STEPS

1. Pour the dried yeast into the plastic bottle.
2. Add some warm water to the bottle. Then add a teaspoon of sugar and swirl the bottle around.
3. Place the balloon over the mouth of the bottle so that it is covered and there are no leaks.
4. Place the bottle and balloon on a warm windowsill or keep the bottle in a bowl of warm water.
5. Watch the balloon "magically" blow up!

Now that's what I need at my next birthday party. Twenty or thirty bottles of this stuff to take the hard work out of blowing up balloons!

Materials
- 1 packet of dried yeast
- warm water
- sugar
- teaspoon
- clear plastic bottle
- balloon

Did You Know?
This seems like a great trick but it is not really magic. By adding sugar and warmth to the yeast, the yeast, which is a plant, grows and produces a gas called carbon dioxide. The carbon dioxide in the bottle rises and fills up the balloon.

71 Barney Banana

Trick your friends into thinking you have created a new type of banana.

Materials
- banana
- long sewing needle

STEPS

1. Carefully push the needle into one of the edges of the banana. Push it all the way to the other side of the banana but do not push it through the skin on the other side.
2. Move the needle up and down. This will slice the banana inside.
3. Keep doing this all the way along the banana, leaving about a finger space between each hole. Only put the needle in one side of the banana or your friends may see even these tiny holes.
4. Now peel the banana for your friends. They will be amazed that inside is a beautifully sliced banana.

Did You Know?
This will not work with any other fruit. It is only because bananas are so soft that this works. Bananas are made up of thousands and thousands of tiny hairs and this is why they are so soft.

72 Fruit or Vegetable?

Classify some foods as either fruits or vegetables.

STEPS

1. Cut all the foods in half.
2. Look at the inside and see if you can spot a seed.
3. If there is a seed then the food is classified as a fruit. Any surprises?

Hmmm. SEEDS! That's a fruit then!

Materials
- different foods—tomato, carrot, avocado, orange, potato, strawberry
- chopping board
- knife

Did You Know?

Because they have seeds, tomatoes and avocados are classed as fruit, not vegetables. We might think of fruit as sweet foods because of the natural sugar in them and not something we would eat with cheese in our sandwich. As you can see, this is not always so.

---

73 When is a Fruit a Berry?

Fruit can be sorted into three groups.

STEPS

1. Cut all the fruit in half.
2. Look very carefully at the inside of the fruit and find the seeds.
3. Sort the fruit into three groups—a group with one large hard seed in the middle; a group where there are many seeds throughout the fruit; and a group where there are some seeds surrounded by a core.

These are the three groups used to classify fruit.

Materials
- different fruit—orange, grape, apricot, plum, apple, and pear
- chopping board
- knife

Did You Know?

The three classifications of fruit are:
1) Drupes—which have one hard seed in the middle, such as peaches.
2) Berries—where the seeds are throughout the fruit, such as oranges and raspberries.
3) Pomes—which have many seeds in a core, such as pears and apples.

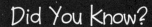

74 Making Ginger Ale

Make ginger ale.

STEPS

1. Ask for help to boil 12 cups of water in a large pan. Add 1½ tablespoons of ginger, juice from the lime, 1½ cups of sugar, and 1½ tablespoons of cream of tartar.
2. Leave the mixture to cool until it is just warm, then add the yeast and mix with the spoon until the yeast is dissolved. Place the lid on the pan and leave for six hours.
3. Have someone hold the sieve over the measuring cup and pour the mixture into the measuring cup. Throw away whatever is left in the sieve.
4. Place the funnel in the top of the bottle. Slowly pour the mixture into the bottle. Do not fill it all the way up.
5. Put the lid on tightly and place it in the refrigerator. Leave it for two days, and then it is ready to drink.

Did You Know?

When mixed with sugar and heated, the yeast produces a gas called carbon dioxide that makes the mixture fizzy. The gas is what makes the bubbles in the ginger ale. This is called "carbonation," which is why fizzy drinks are called carbonated drinks.

I'm not that crazy about the ginger ale ... but I do like the carbon dioxide bubbles.

Materials
- measuring cup
- large pan with a lid
- water
- 1½ tbsp. powdered ginger
- tablespoon
- ¼ lime
- 1½ cups sugar
- 1½ tbsp. cream of tartar
- dried yeast
- sieve
- funnel
- mixing spoon
- 12 cup bottle with lid

---

75 Lemon Floaties

Can a lemon float in water?

STEPS

1. Fill the bowl with water. Place the lemon in the water and watch it float.
2. Cut the lemon into pieces.
3. Now put the lemon pieces in the water. Watch what happens.

Materials
- lemon
- bowl of water
- knife
- chopping board

Did You Know?

The lemon fills with water after it is cut and sinks because it is too heavy. The skin on the lemon is waterproof and protects the lemon from the weather when it is growing on the tree.

76 Mold Mania

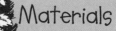

Grow different colored molds on different foods.

STEPS

1. Cut the food into pieces each about the size of a coin.
2. Dip each piece of food in water.
3. Lay the container on its side and put the food inside. Make sure each piece is touching the others, but do not put all the food on top of each other.
4. Put the lid on tightly and seal the container with the tape. Place the container of food scraps in a place where no one will bump it (or eat it!).
5. Observe the food every day. In the first two or three days there will probably be very little change. Soon you will start to get mold of many different colors.
6. After a few days some of the food will start to rot. Leave it for two weeks and see what happens. After that you will need to throw the container and scraps out. Don't open it. Mold can be dangerous for people to breathe in.

Materials
- clear container— glass jar or plastic container with a lid
- tape
- water
- food scraps such as bread, vegetables, fruit, cheese. (Do not use any meat, chicken, or fish.)
- knife
- chopping board

Did You Know?
The mold that grows in the container is a type of fungus. Mushrooms are another type of fungus. Unlike plants that grow from seeds, mold grows from spores floating around in the air, which grow on damp food and turn into mold.

77 Making a Compost Bin

Make a compost bin to keep at home.

STEPS

1. Make sure the bin has holes in the bottom. Fill the bin with the newspapers and other things, including the straw or leaves, making sure that it is moist.
2. Get some worms from your yard. Dig up the dirt and find some worms to put in your compost bin.
3. You must feed the worms. They can have food such as fruit and vegetables and bread. Note: Do not use meat, chicken, milk (and other dairy foods), or eggs.
4. Put the lid on. Keep the bin outside on the ground in the yard.
5. Make sure your compost bin is always moist. If not, add more water. Keep the lid on because it will get smelly.

Materials
- large plastic bin with lid and holes in the bottom
- moist old newspapers
- worms
- straw, sawdust, shredded leaves
- food scraps (see note in Step 3)

Did You Know?
Compost makes a great fertilizer for your garden. Fertilizer helps keep your plants healthy by feeding them extra nutrients. It is important for everyone to learn about recycling.

78 Compost is My Home

Inspect the creatures that live in compost.

"Will you look at the yummy bugs in this compost."

"Don't try this at home ... unless you're a frog."

Materials
- rotting leaves from a compost bin
- large clear jar
- plastic funnel
- rubber gloves
- kitchen foil
- desk lamp
- magnifying glass

Did You Know?
Light from lamps causes heat. In this experiment the creatures can move and the leaves can't, so the bugs will try to move away from the light and farther into the funnel where they fall down the slope into the jar.

STEPS
1. Put on the rubber gloves. Collect some rotting leaves from the compost bin. Do not touch the leaves without the gloves.
2. Place the funnel on top of the jar. Loosely place the rotting leaves inside the funnel.
3. Cover the jar with kitchen foil. The whole jar must be covered to block out all the light.
4. Place the desk lamp so the light is shining directly onto the jar of leaves.
5. Leave for about an hour then use the magnifying glass to examine what is in the jar.

79 The Oldest Tree

How can you measure the age of a tree?

Materials
- large ball of string
- scissors
- tape
- measuring tape
- pencil
- piece of paper
- a friend

STEPS
1. Find some big trees in your backyard or at the park.
2. Cut a piece of string about 3 ft (1 m) long (you may not need all of this or you might need a longer piece, depending how thick the tree trunk is).
3. Stick one end of the string on the tree and wrap it around the trunk. Match the other end up to the end that is stuck to the tree. Use your scissors to cut it off.
4. Remove the string and use the measuring tape to measure the distance around the tree (called the girth). Record how big each tree is on your piece of paper.
5. Do this for as many trees as you can find. Ask the person with you if they can tell you what type of tree you are measuring.
6. After you have finished measuring, see which tree has the longest piece of string. Most of the time this is the oldest tree.

"Well, you must be the oldest tree in the yard. How old are you? 120?"

"No, 121 actually."

Did You Know?
Every year trees grow a new layer of bark around them. This means the more layers of bark, the wider the tree becomes. The tree gets wider and wider as it gets older and older. If you ever see a tree cut down, look at the trunk. You can see a swirly pattern, starting with a small circle in the middle and lots of rings around this. These rings are the layers of bark. The more rings the trunk has, the older the tree.

80 Grasses

Find different types of grasses in your yard.

Materials
- paper
- pencil

It may not look like grass ... but this is my front lawn.

STEPS

1. Do this activity at a park or at home.
2. See how many different types of grass you can find. Remember if you are near a pond there will be different types near the water.
3. Sort them and then list them in order of the most common in the area to the least common.

Did You Know?
Grasses come in all different types. Like trees, some are soft and some are hard. Near water, grasses tend to be a lot harder.

---

81 Bark Rubbing

Look at the different patterns of bark on trees.

Materials
- large sheet of white paper
- crayons

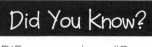

STEPS

1. Place the paper against the trunk of the tree.
2. Lay the crayon on its side and rub it on the paper. You should start to see a pattern appear on the paper. If it is not working you might need to press harder or you might be pressing too hard.
3. When you have finished with one tree, write on the paper with the rubbing what type of tree it is (if you don't know, ask someone).
4. Try different trees using different crayons.

Did You Know?
Different trees have different bark. You can see from your rubbings that some trees have smooth bark and some have rough bark.

82 Bark Detective

Materials
- magnifying glass
- trees

Find what is hiding in tree bark.

STEPS

1. Find a tree with a thick trunk.
2. Look for cracks in the bark. Use the magnifying glass to look for insects hiding in the bark.
3. Find places on the tree where the bark is peeling. Pull back the bark very carefully and look for insects that live in the decaying bark.
4. At the bottom of the tree there is often green, powdery moss where other creatures live.

Did You Know?

Bark is the home of many insects. We know that birds often live in the branches of trees but bark makes a nice, sheltered home for insects.

---

83 Leaf Rubbing

Materials
- different types of leaves
- paper
- crayons

Inspect the different parts of leaves and make a picture.

One guess as to what leaf I chose for my leaf rubbing?

STEPS

1. Place the leaves on the table.
2. Put the paper on top of the leaves.
3. Lay the crayon on its side and slide over the paper. If this is not working try pressing harder or softer.
4. Use different leaves and different crayons to make a colorful picture.

Did You Know?

Inside the leaf you will be able to see lines on the paper. Down the middle of each leaf you will see a bigger line. This is the vein that attaches each leaf to the stem of the plant and brings water into the leaves. The smaller lines move the water around the leaf.

84 Crazy Leaves

Look at the different shapes of leaves.

Materials
- paper
- pencil
- tape

STEPS

1. Do this experiment at the park or in your backyard.
2. Pick leaves from trees. (If there are leaves on the ground under the tree, try to use those.) You may like to note the trees where you picked these leaves.
3. Sort the leaves into matching shapes and stick them to the paper.
4. Find out if there are any similarities between the shapes of the leaves from big trees or small trees. Which leaves appear to have more insects living on them?

Did You Know?
The maple leaf is so special that it appears on the Canadian flag. Not only is the leaf from this tree an interesting shape but the maple tree also produces that yummy maple syrup you put on your pancakes!

85 Tree Encyclopedia

Make a book of photos of different trees in your yard or park.

Materials
- digital camera
- small notebook
- pencil
- guidebook on trees (you can borrow this from your local library)
- large scrapbook
- glue stick

STEPS

Note: This experiment is fantastic if you make bark and leaf rubbings as well. You can find these at Experiments 81 and 83.

1. Choose a tree in a park or your backyard and make notes about it. This is a good chance to make a bark and leaf rubbing to add to your information.
2. Take a close-up photograph of the tree. Take some from different angles and some close-ups of the bark. Have the pictures saved into a computer and print them for your scrapbook.
3. Visit different places with different trees. Use your guidebook to help you identify each tree.
4. Stick the photographs into the scrapbook. Under the photograph write the name of the tree and any information you have discovered. Sticking your bark and leaf rubbings in with the photographs makes an interesting scrapbook.

Did You Know?
The smaller lines on a leaf move the water around.

"I have been called a biology nerd, but it's not true."

"Will you just look at the bark on that tree!"

86 Pressed Leaves & Flowers

Make a leaf and flower press to preserve leaves and flowers.

Materials
- old newspaper
- heavy books
- freshly picked leaves
- fresh flowers

STEPS

1. Collect as many different leaves and flowers as you can from one place. You might like to collect them from many locations to compare the differences. Make sure they are not wet.

2. Start with all the leaves and flowers from one place. Put a book on the bottom then cover it with a sheet of newspaper. Place some of the leaves or flowers on top of the newspaper. Make sure that they are not touching each other and are not on top of each other.

3. Place another sheet of newspaper and then a book on top of the flowers or leaves. Repeat layers of newspaper, flowers, newspaper, and books, making a tower with the books, until you have run out of leaves and flowers.

4. If you have things from different places make another pile with the books and newspaper again and write where they came from.

5. Wait at least four weeks (if not longer) until the leaves are flat and dry.

6. There are many things you can make with your pressed plant material: a picture or cards for your friends.

Did You Know?
The newspaper absorbs all of the water and moisture from the leaves and flowers. This stops them from rotting after all that time.

---

87 Making Potpourri

Make potpourri using all types of flowers.

Materials
- different types of flowers (roses and lavender are great)
- scissors
- heavy books
- paper

STEPS

1. Collect all the flowers you are going to use. If they have long stems cut the stem off, leaving about a thumb length below the flower.

2. Place a book on the ground or table. On top of the book place a sheet of paper and then some flowers. You must make sure that they are not touching each other and are not on top of each other or they will not dry out properly.

3. On top of the flowers place another sheet of paper and then a book. Repeat layers of paper, flowers, paper, and books, making a tower with the books, until you have run out of flowers.

4. Place the "flower press" you have made in a space where it will not be knocked over.

5. Wait at least four weeks until the flowers have dried out.

6. When the flowers are dried, pull the petals off all the flowers and mix them in a bowl. You will have a lovely smelling potpourri.

Did You Know?
Flowers smell nice because of the oil in their petals. Every flower smells differently because they all produce different oils. These oils are often used in soaps and candles to make them smell nice. Visit your local florist and smell all the different flowers. Which ones do you like the best?

88 Purple Celery

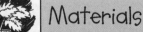

Create purple celery.

STEPS

1. Cut the celery into pieces of the same length. Chop off the bottom, and at 4 in (10 cm) below the leaves.
2. Fill each glass with an equal amount of water.
3. Add 10 drops of red and 10 drops of blue food dye to each jar.
4. Place one piece of celery in each glass.
5. After one hour remove the first piece of celery from the jar. Has anything changed? Peel the round part and measure how far up the celery the dye has gone.
6. Remove the celery from the jars at different times—after two hours, four hours, six hours, eight hours, and overnight (you have six glasses). Peel, and measure the dye. Observe the difference to the celery after each time interval and make notes in a journal.

Materials
- 6 long pieces of celery
- chopping board
- knife
- red and blue food dye
- 6 drinking glasses
- water
- vegetable peeler
- ruler

Just like people, plants need water to survive. Plants get water from the dirt through their roots. Inside the plants are capillaries that allow the water to travel through the

Did You Know?

plant. You can see from the celery that over a period of time the plant draws water up through its capillaries all the way through its system.

89 Stemless Flowers

See what happens to a flower with no stem.

Materials
- 2 fresh flowers
- scissors

STEPS

1. Use the scissors to cut the stem off one of the flowers.
2. Leave both flowers in a safe spot.
3. Check after an hour and note the difference between them. What happens after 2–3 days?

Did You Know?

The stem of the flower holds water. It draws water up when flowers are in a vase to keep the flower petals moist. Even when it is out of water the stem still holds some water. Without the stem the flower has no way of getting water and dies much faster than the flower with the stem.

90 Plants and Air

Can plants grow without fresh air?

STEPS

1. Wearing the rubber gloves, half fill the jar with soil.
2. Plant the seedling in the soil in the jar, making sure the roots are covered.
3. Lightly water the seedling and screw the lid on tightly.
4. Fill the pot with soil until it almost reaches the top.
5. Plant the second seedling, covering the roots.
6. Place the pot on the saucer of water.
7. Put both the jar and the potted plant in a sunny place and leave for a few days.

Help me out here and take the lid off this jar. I need some fresh carbon dioxide!

Materials
- 2 seedlings
- soil
- pot
- saucer
- jar with a lid
- rubber gloves
- water

Did You Know?

Without air, plants cannot survive. Plants need the gas called carbon dioxide from the air. We also need the plants to keep the air healthy for people and animals. Plants pass out oxygen from their leaves. Oxygen is the part of air that people and animals need to help them breathe. Without plants there would not be enough oxygen in the air for us!

---

91 Plants and Soil

Can plants grow without soil?

STEPS

1. Wearing the rubber gloves, fill one of the small pots with soil until it almost reaches the top.
2. Plant one of the seedlings in this pot with the soil, making sure the roots are covered.
3. Place the other seedling in a pot with no soil.
4. Put both pots on a saucer of water.
5. Place in a sunny spot and leave for a few days.

Materials
- 2 seedlings
- soil
- 2 small pots
- 2 saucers
- rubber gloves
- water

Did You Know?

Soil plays an important part in helping a plant grow. Soil contains lots of nutrients and minerals that help the plant grow. It also allows the roots of the plant to grow and hold the plant up, which is especially important for big plants such as trees. Their roots are enormous and act like a boat anchor to hold the tree in place.

92 Plants and Water

Do plants need water to grow?

STEPS

1. Wearing the rubber gloves, fill all three pots with soil almost to the top.
2. Plant one seedling in each pot, making sure the roots of the plant are well covered. Place a pot on each of the saucers.
3. On the first pot use the marker to write "no water." Place this pot in a sunny spot and do not water.
4. On the second pot write "cola" (or whatever drink you are using). Fill the saucer with the drink and place in a sunny spot.
5. On the third pot write "water." Fill the saucer with water and place in a sunny spot.
6. Leave your plants. You will need to make sure they are damp and if they are not, add more water or cola, depending on which plant it is.

Ever seen a hyperactive Petunia?

Well, stick around because you're going to see one!

Materials
- 3 seedlings
- soil
- 3 small pots
- 3 saucers
- rubber gloves
- water
- carbonated drink
- permanent marker

Did You Know?

Water is good for you and for plants. Because water comes from under the Earth many minerals have been dissolved in the water. These minerals are necessary to help the plants grow. Without them plants will die. All the extra things in cola, like sugar and additives, are not good for the plant.

93 Brown Light? Clear Light?

See if plants can grow in different colored light.

STEPS

1. Use the scissors to cut off the top part of the bottles.
2. Wearing the rubber gloves, fill the small pots with soil almost to the top. Put the plants in the pots, making sure you cover the roots.
3. Place the pots on the saucers of water, then put in a sunny spot.
4. Turn the two bottle bottoms upside down over the plants.
5. Keep watering your plants during this activity. Observe your plants every few days and take note of the differences.

Did You Know?

Although the plant in the brown bottle is getting light, the colored plastic acts as a "filter." This means that some of the sunlight is blocked by the brown color and this plant does not get as much sunlight as the one in the clear plastic bottle. This is why the one in the clear plastic bottle is growing faster and is larger.

Materials
- 2 small plants
- 2 small pots
- 2 saucers
- 2 plastic bottles— one clear and one brown
- scissors
- soil
- rubber gloves
- water

94 Undercover Leaves

Observe how leaves change color when they do not receive natural light.

STEPS

1. Count the number of leaves on the plant. You will cover half of them with the kitchen foil and half with the plastic wrap.
2. Fold pieces of kitchen foil over half of the number of leaves on the plant. Leave space for air to get in and out.
3. Now use the plastic wrap to cover the other leaves, again leaving space for the leaves to breathe.
4. Leave the plant in a sunny spot. Each day observe the changes to the color of the leaves.

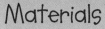

Materials
- small potted plant with large leaves
- kitchen foil
- plastic wrap
- water

Did You Know?
Sunlight is not only important to help plants grow but it also helps give plants their colors. It helps the leaves produce chlorophyll, which makes them go green.

95 Plants From Other Plants

You can use a plant cutting to grow a new plant.

STEPS

1. Cut a stem from a plant such as a begonia. Remember to make sure there are at least two leaves on the cutting. If there are any flowers on your cutting, take them off.
2. Wearing the rubber gloves, fill the pot with soil. Push a hole in the soil as deep as your thumb.
3. Place the cutting in the soil and carefully cover the bottom.
4. Leave the plant on a saucer and cover with the plastic bag. Keep it in a sunny place and remember to water it.

Boy! It's getting really warm and steamy in here. But hey ... I think I'm sprouting another shoot!

Materials
- scissors
- plant cutting such as begonia (with at least two leaves on it)
- small pot
- soil
- saucer
- water
- plastic bag

Did You Know?
The plastic bag acts like a greenhouse in this activity. It keeps the plant warm and damp and encourages it to grow more quickly.

96 Salty Bean Sprouts

What is the effect of salt in the soil when trying to grow plants?

Materials
- 2 clear plastic cups
- cotton wool
- salt
- water
- bean sprout seeds
- marker

STEPS

1. Cover the bottom of each cup with cotton wool.
2. In one cup sprinkle the cotton wool with salt. Write on the cup "salt added."
3. Put about five bean sprout seeds on top of the cotton wool in each cup, then add a little water.
4. Place in a brightly lit window and leave for a few days. Observe the cups and make note of which sprouts are growing first and faster.

Did You Know?

Salt comes from water and because there is water in the soil there is also salt in the soil. Salt makes it very difficult for plants to grow (you can see this in your experiment). In some places, if the water underground comes up too high, the salt level in the soil is also too high, making it impossible to grow plants, even for farmers.

97 Grass Heads

Turn old stockings into creatures.

Materials
- grass or alfalfa seeds
- old stockings
- scissors
- cotton wool
- saucer
- ribbon, old buttons, yarn

STEPS

1. You will only need the end of the stocking where the toes go. Cut the stocking, leaving about 12 in (30 cm).
2. Pour grass seeds into the stocking so they fill the part where the toes would normally be, then fill the stocking with cotton wool until the stocking is a ball shape.
3. Tie the stocking tightly around the cotton wool. Use the scissors to cut off any extra stocking material.
4. Turn the stocking so that the grass seeds are on the top.
5. You can now decorate the stocking to make it look like a face. When the grass grows it will become the hair.
6. Place the stocking on a saucer of water. Place in a sunny spot.
7. The seeds will take a few days to start growing. Make sure the stocking is always damp and if not, water it.

Did You Know?

Grass seeds and alfalfa seeds do not need soil to start to grow, like a lot of other plants do. Unlike other plants these seeds grow quickly and do not need the nutrients provided by soil to begin with. They do need to be kept moist in order to germinate and grow.

98 Is a Spider an Insect?

Classification of insects and spiders.

STEPS

1. Count the number of legs on the spider.
2. There should be eight.
3. Insects have six legs. So a spider is not an insect.

Materials
- dead spider (ask an adult to make sure) or a toy spider. Do not pick up a live spider—it may be venomous.

Did You Know?
An insect is a creature with six legs. Although a spider is not an insect they do share some of the same body parts. Both insects and spiders do not have a separate head. Their head is part of their body called the "thorax." The bottom part of their body is called the "abdomen."

99 Buzzy Bees

What attracts bees?

Did You Know?
Bees are attracted to the sweetness of the sugar and the carbonated drink. A bright color also brings more bees to the flowers. You should have observed the bees being drawn toward the colored flowers rather than the black and white cardboard and to the caps with the sugar and carbonated drink.

Materials
- 5 pieces of strong cardboard, 1 black, 1 white, and 3 different colors
- drinking straws
- water
- scissors
- tape or adhesive putty
- 4 plastic lids from small jars or soft drink bottles
- sugar
- carbonated drink (e.g. cola)
- salt
- notebook
- pencil

STEPS

1. Cut the cardboard into the shape of flowers with large petals. Make five different colored flowers.
2. Using the scissors, cut four small slits in one end of five drinking straws. Push this end onto the back of the flowers so it makes a star shape. Use the tape to attach the straw to the cardboard. Repeat so that you have five flowers on the straws.
3. Mix a tiny amount of sugar with water so that it forms a sticky paste and place in one of the lids. Repeat with the salt. Repeat with the carbonated drink.
4. Roll up balls of tape or adhesive putty and place one ball in the middle of four of the posterboard flowers.
5. Stick the lids on the tape or adhesive putty. Two flowers will not have a cap.
6. Place the flowers outside. Observe and record which colored flower the bees are most attracted to and what is in the cap on that flower.
7. Now switch the caps around to another flower. Record the results.

100 Catching Ants

Which food attracts the most ants?

Materials
- small amount of sugar (a teaspoon is enough)
- small piece of apple
- piece of bread
- potato
- chopping board
- knife

STEPS
1. Cut the food into pieces.
2. Place some of each one in different places around the yard.
3. Watch to see which one of these foods attracts the most ants.

I think I'd better hop off to another part of the garden before these ants like me as much as this piece of apple!

Did You Know?
Ants are attracted to the apple. The sweetness of the apple gives off a strong scent that attracts the ants. The ants are also attracted to the sugar.

---

101 Make an Ant Colony

You can build an ant colony.

Materials
- glass jar
- dirt
- kitchen foil
- old stocking material
- scissors
- spoon
- honey
- leaves
- rubber gloves

STEPS
1. Wearing the rubber gloves, fill the jar with dirt. Lightly water the dirt and place the leaves on top.
2. Wrap the foil around the outside of the jar and secure it in place with tape.
3. Go outside and put some honey on the spoon. Put the spoon on the ground near some ants and wait for the ants to come to the honey. When you have ants on the spoon, gently tap the spoon on top of the jar so that the ants and honey fall on top of the leaves.
4. Place the old stocking over the top of the jar and use the rubber band to hold it in place.
5. Feed the ants each day with fresh fruit and leaves. Make sure the dirt is damp.
6. Keep the ant colony in a cool place, away from the sun.
7. After a few days remove the foil and look at the jar. You will see that the ants have made winding tunnels through the dirt.

Did You Know?
Ants live in colonies. Each of the ants has a special job. The queen ant lays the eggs and the other ants find food and bring it to the nest of the queen ant. When they find food they drag it back to the nest, leaving a scent behind, so that the other ants can follow the smell to find more food.

What a great place for an ant's nest! There's enough room in here for 200,000 of us. Each with our own bedroom!

102 Create a New Insect

Use your knowledge of insects to create a new insect.

Materials
- old boxes and containers
- tape
- paint
- markers
- newspaper
- scissors
- glue
- buttons, pipe cleaners,
- popsicle sticks

STEPS

1. Think about all the things you know about insects—their body parts, their colors used for camouflage, and the number of legs they have.
2. Stick the boxes and containers together with the tape to create a new insect.
3. Spread the newspaper on the floor and paint the creature.
4. Leave the paint to dry and then decorate it with the markers and other things that you have collected.

Did You Know?
Using imagination is a vital part of science to explore and discover, but it's the facts that are found out that is important.

---

103 Leaf Eaters

Observe which creatures eat particular leaves.

Materials
- 3 small jars
- plastic wrap
- 3 rubber bands
- insects from your backyard or park
- different kinds of leaves (3 each)—if you already know which ones are being eaten pick some of these

STEPS

1. Collect the insects in a jar and take them home.
2. Place an insect in each jar. Choose one type of leaf at a time. Place one leaf in each jar.
3. Cover the jars with plastic wrap and secure with a rubber band. Make sure there are small holes in the cover so that the animals can breathe.
4. Leave the jars for a while. Observe which animals are eating the leaf.
5. Choose a different type and change the leaves over. You can keep repeating this experiment until you have tried all the leaves.

Did You Know?
Different insects will eat different leaves. Insects are a bit like people—we don't all like the same foods and nor do they.

104 Attracting Butterflies

Grow a beautiful garden that attracts butterflies.

STEPS

1. Wearing the rubber gloves, fill the pot with soil until it almost reaches the top.
2. Plant the pansies in the pot, making sure you leave lots of room between each plant so that they have space to grow.
3. Make sure that the roots are covered.
4. Place the pot outside in a sunny spot and make sure to keep watering it.
5. The flowers will attract beautiful butterflies.

Materials
- small flowering plants, such as pansies
- watering can
- large pot (if you don't have a back yard)
- soil
- rubber gloves

Did You Know?
Butterflies and birds are attracted to flowers because they feed off them. They are attracted by the nectar on the plant which you can see them drinking. The nectar on these plants is very sweet for the animals.

---

105 Making a Butterfly

Hatch caterpillars into butterflies.

STEPS

Note: When choosing leaves for this experiment look for ones that have been eaten by caterpillars already. This way you know they are leaves the caterpillars like to eat.

1. Fill the jar with water and place the branches in the jar and put it inside the aquarium.
2. Place the caterpillars on the leaves.
3. Put the lid on and use the tape to hold it in place.
4. Leave the aquarium. This experiment will take several weeks to complete. You will need to watch the leaves. When they are eaten replace them with fresh branches from the same plant. When the caterpillars become fat they will make their cocoon. The cocoon will begin to move when the butterfly is ready to come out.

Materials
- glass aquarium with a glass lid
- wide tape
- glass jar
- water
- leaves on branches
- caterpillars

Did You Know?
The correct name for the caterpillar in this process is the larva. It produces the pupa (the cocoon) and from this hatches a butterfly. Butterflies lay eggs. Can you guess what hatches from a butterfly's egg? Yes, that's right, a caterpillar!

106 How Slow Is a Snail?

Slow as a snail!

STEPS

1. Place the stone on the ground. This marks where the snail starts.
2. Put the snail next to the rock and start the stopwatch.
3. Time for two minutes. After two minutes use the measuring tape to measure from the small rock to the snail and record the result.
4. To work out how fast a snail moves per hour multiply how far the snail traveled in two minutes by thirty.
5. If you have more than one snail you may like to repeat the experiment and compare them. Are some snails faster than others?

Materials
- at least one snail (snails come out after the rain or at night)
- measuring tape
- watch or stopwatch
- calculator (or paper and pencil)
- small stone

Did You Know?
Snails leave a slimy trail behind them when they move. This slime helps them move along the ground.

---

107 How Strong is a Snail?

How strong is a snail?

STEPS

1. Poke a small hole in each side of the matchbox.
2. Cut a piece of cotton thread about 8 in (20 cm) long. Thread one end through a hole and tie. Repeat on the opposite side. You now have a cart with a handle.
3. Carefully loop the cotton over the snail's shell so the matchbox is behind the snail.
4. See if the snail can still move and pull the matchbox.
5. Add one stone at a time. See how many the snail can pull.
6. If you have several snails you might compare which is the strongest by seeing which snail can pull the most stones in its cart.

Materials
- snails
- empty matchboxes
- scissors
- cotton thread or fine yarn
- small stones

Did You Know?
If you shine a flashlight on concrete at night, you may see some shiny trails left behind by snails.

108 Wriggling Worms

What makes worms wriggle?

Materials
- worms in a container of dirt
- dry dirt
- small lamp or flashlight
- ice cream stick
- ice cubes

STEPS

1. Spread the newspaper out on a table.
2. Tip the worms out of their container onto the newspaper. Pick them out of the dirt.
3. You are going to use the different materials to see how the worms respond. First, push them gently with the ice cream stick to see their response.
4. Next, shine the flashlight on them. Then put them on the dry dirt and see what happens. Finally, place them on top of the cube of ice.
5. When you have finished put the dirt back into the container and watch the worms crawl back into the dirt.

Did You Know?

Worms always live underground. They like a damp, dark environment to live in. Although they like moisture, the ice is much too cold for them.

109 Pond in a Jar

Many creatures live in ponds.

Materials
- large jar with a lid
- stick, slightly shorter than the jar
- small spade
- plastic bottle
- magnifying glass
- pond

STEPS

1. Use the spade to put mud from the pond in the bottom of your jar.
2. Carefully take some small plants from the water (ask an adult to help you) and plant them in the mud.
3. Half fill the bottle with water from the pond. Pour it in against the side of the jar.
4. Place the stick in the jar and replace the lid.
5. Leave in a shady place and add water if you notice your "pond" drying up.
6. Use your magnifying glass to observe what is growing and moving inside the jar and see if you can identify some of the living things.

EEK!! I've stayed in some ponds that had water that color.

The stick is there because some of the creatures that live in ponds don't always stay in the water. Can you think of any animals that you know of that live on land and water? Frogs are one of them and you might find them at the pond.

Did You Know?

110 Feeding the Birds

Make food that will attract birds.

STEPS

1. Ask an adult to melt the fat for you in the microwave oven or a pan.
2. In the mixing bowl put half a cup of each ingredient. Mix them together, then add the fat. The mixture should be like soggy cereal, but not too runny. If there is too much liquid from the fat, add more oats.
3. Tie a big knot in the end of the string and put the knotted end in the bottom of the cup. Hang the string over the side of the cup.
4. Make sure the string does not fall into the cup. Pour the oat mixture into it, then push down hard so that there is no air.
5. Move the string into the middle of the cup and put it in the refrigerator to set.
6. When the mixture is solid, push on the bottom of the cup and the mixture should come out as a "bird cake." If you cannot get it out, try pulling on the string or ask for help to run warm water over the outside of the cup for a short time.
7. Tie the string to a branch in a tree and wait for the birds to come.

Did You Know?

This bird cake will attract different types of birds. Find a book about different birds and about which ones are eating your food.

Materials
- animal fat
- oats
- breadcrumbs
- chopped nuts
- seeds such as pumpkin seeds
- long piece of string
- plastic cup
- mixing bowl
- spoon

Note: You can use commercial birdseed in this experiment in place of the breadcrumbs, seeds, and nuts. You will still need the oats to make the mixture thick.

---

111 Making a Bird Feeder

Build a bird feeder that will attract birds.

STEPS

1. Cut the top half off the milk carton. You must make sure that the bottom part (that you are going to use) is clean and dry.
2. Use the scissors to poke a hole in each side of the carton. The holes must be near the top of the carton and in the middle of each side.
3. Cut two pieces of string the same length. Thread one end of the string through a hole and tie it tightly. Now take the other end of this piece of string and tie it to the hole on the opposite side of the carton. Repeat with the other piece of string, tying it to the other holes.
4. Now fill your bird feeder with birdseed and take it outside. Hang the feeder over a branch on a tree and watch the birds come to feed.

Materials
- empty milk carton
- string
- scissors
- birdseed

I'm waiting for someone to build a larger, heavier bird feeder for larger, heavier birds.

Boy, that birdseed looks good!

Did You Know?

You may find that some birds are too big for your bird feeder. Next time you could use something larger or ask an adult to build one out of wood.

112 Observing Birds Feeding

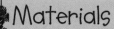

Materials
- pencil
- notebook

See how birds use their beaks to feed.

STEPS

1. Sit in your backyard or park and watch the birds.
2. Observe how they eat. Some birds will open their beaks first while some will stick their beaks into the food.
3. Draw a beak on your paper and write how a bird with a beak that shape eats.

I can only wonder what you've developed a beak like that for, my feathered friend!

Did You Know?
Birds in different places will have different shaped beaks based on the food available.

---

113 Making a Birdbath

Materials
- large plastic container (an old ice cream container is fine)
- permanent markers
- water
- old bread crusts

Make a birdbath.

STEPS

1. Use the permanent markers to decorate your container or birdbath. Draw flowers and bugs so that your birdbath looks pretty in the yard.
2. Fill the container with water.
3. Put some small pieces of bread in the water. This will give the birds something to eat.
4. Place the container outside, in a tree if you can. Wait and see who visits.

Pass me another piece of that soggy, wet bread if there's any of it still floating in the tub. There's nothing better than a piece of soggy bread in the tub is there?

Did You Know?
Rainbow lorikeets only have one mating partner for life!

114 Bird Calls

Record the sounds of birds.

Materials
- small tape recorder
- batteries
- tape
- notebook
- pencil

STEPS
1. Put the batteries in the tape player and make sure you know how to record on it.
2. Walk around outside and record the bird sounds you hear. Make notes in your notebook of any birds you know. This helps you remember which birds were making the sounds.
3. This is a fun experiment to do with a friend to see if they can identify the sounds of any birds. It can be quite tricky.

Hello Cocky! Hello Cocky! Cocky want a cracker. Clever Cocky. Pretty boy, Cocky. Hello Cocky! Hello Cocky!

I may not have quite enough tape to complete this project.

Did You Know?
Some birds, such as cockatoos, can be taught to say some words. Say "Hello Cocky!" to a cockatoo and often it will say "Hello Cocky!" back.

---

115 Making a Bird Caller

Make a bird caller to attract the attention of birds.

Materials
- drinking straw
- scissors

STEPS
1. Squeeze one end of a drinking straw flat.
2. Use the scissors to cut this flattened end into a point. (For this to work the pointed end must be very flat.)
3. Put the pointed end in your mouth and blow hard. A very funny noise should come out.
4. You may notice birds looking at you wondering what type of bird you are!

This is the call of the Blue-breasted Fairy-wren.

What's that terrible squeaking noise? It sounds like someone blowing through a plastic drinking straw.

Did You Know?
Birds are able to sing two different notes at the same time by controlling both sides of their tracheae independently.

116 Bird Beaks

Experiment with different types of bird "beaks."

Materials
- kitchen tongs
- tweezers
- clothes pegs
- toothpicks

STEPS

1. Go into the backyard or the park to do this experiment.
2. Using each of the materials ("beaks") see what things you can pick up.
3. Make a list of the things you were able to pick up with each "beak."

Did You Know?

It is impossible for a small sparrow to pick up a fish, whereas a pelican, which has a large beak, can take a whole fish in its mouth.

---

117 Design a Beak for You!

Design and make a beak to pick up your food.

Materials
- old boxes and containers from food items
- tape
- scissors
- your favorite food

STEPS

1. You will need to think carefully about your chosen food—is it soft, crumbly, or hard? If you poke something into it will it fall apart? Is it big or small? Is it wet or dry? All these things will change how you design your beak.
2. Decide on a design and draw it on paper.
3. Use the materials to make your beak. Use lots of tape so that it is really strong.
4. When it is finished, test your beak by trying to see if you can pick up your food. Yummy!

Did You Know?

Humans don't need beaks. We are lucky enough to have arms and hands to help us to pick up food and eat. Other animals, like squirrels, also pick up their food and hold it to nibble on. They also have strong teeth so they can eat hard foods, like acorns.

118 Animal Activities

Observe the habits of animals.

STEPS

1. Sit where you can see the animal but will not disturb it.
2. Start timing the animal when it begins a new activity. List the activity and for how long it did it in your notebook.
3. The animal may move quickly from one activity to another (like a bee) or it may spend a long time doing one activity (like a cat sleeping).
4. Observe as many animals as you can.
5. Compare your results. Which animals spend more time sleeping? Eating? Running? Flying?

Materials
- notebook
- pencil
- watch or a stopwatch
- animals—observing a pet is a good experiment. If you do not have a pet, ask someone you know if you can observe his or her pet.

Did You Know?

Cats spend most of their day sleeping. In fact, most cats spend around 14 hours a day sleeping. Some animals sleep in the day time and are active at night.

---

119 Guard Dogs

Can you hear as well as a dog?

STEPS

1. Secure the blindfold around your head.
2. If you are playing with a group of people, have them hide around the room. If there is only one other person, have them move to a space in the room.
3. Each person must make a small sound so you can find them. They can also move around the room as you get closer to them.
4. See if you can catch each person.
5. You may play this game where the person hiding does not make a sound at all. You will have to try to hear them walking in order to find them.

Materials
- blindfold
- partner or group of people

Did You Know?

Dogs have an excellent sense of hearing. They can hear sounds before people can. That is why people use dogs as guards to protect them.

120 Footprint Detectives

Materials
- Just your eyes!

Find and identify different animal footprints.

STEPS

1. You can do this experiment at the beach or in a park.
2. Carefully walk around, looking at the ground. See if you can find some footprints.
3. Try to identify the animal these footprints belong to.
4. Look to see whether the footprints are closer or farther apart in some places. Can you guess if the animal was walking or running?

Ok! I think it's time to leave the pond.

Did You Know?

Not all animals leave footprints. Some animals move by sliding and it is harder to know where they have been. When snails slide they leave behind a shiny trail. See if you can come up with a list of animals that slide.

---

121 Footprints

Materials
- plaster of Paris (ready to pour)
- cardboard
- stapler
- beach or park

Make plaster casts of animal footprints.

STEPS

1. Make some cardboard strips and staple the two ends of each together so they make rings.
2. Visit the beach or park.
3. Carefully walk around, looking at the ground. See if you can find some footprints.
4. Place the cardboard ring around the footprint. Pour the plaster into the ring.
5. You will need to wait until the plaster is almost set, then using a stick, write on the back of the plaster the animal the footprint belongs to.
6. When the plaster has set hard, remove the cardboard, lift the plaster up and dust off any extra dirt or sand.

That looks like one of the biggest footprints in the world. And the biggest footprint belongs to an ... ELEPHANT!!

Did You Know?

Elephants have the largest footprint of any animal in the world.

122 Rise Up

Make a loaf of bread.

I can feel a chemical reaction taking place. Can you?

I'm feeling a little fizzy. I think its the carbon dioxide bubbles in the mix!

Materials

- 1 tablespoon sugar
- 1 tablespoon olive oil
- 1 tablespoon yeast
- 1 ¼ cups warm water
- 3 ½ cups flour
- 1 teaspoon salt
- 2 bowls
- 1 baking pan
- pastry brush
- oven
- plastic wrap

STEPS

1. Mix the sugar, oil, yeast, and water in a bowl. It should start to froth.
2. In another bowl, mix the flour and salt.
3. Add the liquids to the solids. Mix and then knead with your hands until smooth and elastic. Brush the ball of dough with oil, and cover with plastic wrap. Leave in a warm place for an hour.
4. Ask an adult to preheat the oven to 425°F (220°C).
5. Roll the dough into a round roll. Brush with butter if you like. Place in a baking pan and bake for 40–60 minutes, or until the top is brown and the loaf sounds "hollow" when tapped. Cool, then eat!

Did You Know?

You can make different kinds of breads by putting different ingredients in the mixture. Multigrain bread is made by putting grains in with the water.

Oh! A little too much yeast in the mix perhaps?

WHY?

Bread has an ingredient called yeast. (Yeast remains dormant until mixed with water.) The warm water activates the yeast, which begins feeding on the sugar. The yeast organisms make carbon dioxide, which is a gas. These bubbles of gas get trapped in the baking dough, so they make the dough "rise."

123 Gumdrop Molecules

Make candy models of molecules.

Materials
- different colored gumdrop
- toothpicks
- bowl

STEPS

1. Give each different atom a color, for example, hydrogen = red, oxygen = yellow, and carbon = green.

2. Make a water molecule (H_2O)—this means that two hydrogen atoms are joined to one oxygen atom inside water. So, join two red pieces of candy to one yellow piece of candy with toothpicks. Put your water molecule in a bowl. Make more!

3. Make a carbon dioxide molecule (CO_2)—this means that two oxygen atoms are joined to one carbon atom. So, join two yellow pieces of candy to one green piece of candy with toothpicks. Put your carbon dioxide molecule in the bowl. Make more!

4. Eat! Which molecule are you eating?

I don't know what sort of molecule this is ... but it looks good enough to eat!

Did You Know?

Water (H_2O) is the most important liquid on Earth. Carbon dioxide (CO_2) is a gas that we breathe out. There are more than 100 different atoms, so you would need more than 100 different colored gumdrops to make every possible molecule!

124 Making Starch

Separate a compound, called starch, from potatoes.

Materials
- 5 large potatoes
- grater
- bowl
- water
- sieve

STEPS

1. Peel the potatoes. Grate them into a bowl.

2. Fill the bowl with water to cover the potatoes. Squeeze the potato with your fingers for several minutes. Leave for half an hour. Repeat the squeezing.

3. Take the potato out of the bowl by pouring the mixture through a sieve and catching the cloudy water in a bowl.

4. Let the cloudy water dry up in a sunny place. What happens?

Did You Know?

A compound is a substance made of two or more elements. You should be left with a white powder in the bowl called starch. Starch is present in many plants, because it is a way they store energy. When you eat potatoes, your body changes this starch back into sugar for energy. This process starts in your mouth, with chemicals in your saliva (spit) breaking down the starch.

CHEMISTRY

CHEMISTRY: THE STUDY OF THE ELEMENTS, THE COMPOUNDS THEY FORM AND THE REACTIONS THEY UNDERGO.

Date:	Experiment:	Notes:

125 Carbon Everywhere

Demonstrate that living things contain carbon.

Materials
- 1 lit candle
- paper
- pencil
- leaves
- sugar
- can lid
- tongs
- bowl of water

STEPS

1. Light the candle. Hold a can lid in the candle flame with the tongs. Cool the lid, then wipe off the black stuff, called soot. This is actually carbon.
2. Make a pencil mark on the paper then rub your finger on it. The black mark on your finger is carbon.
3. Burn paper and leaves. What happens to them?
4. Heat up some sugar on a can lid. What happens to the sugar?

Did You Know?
You were burning some materials that were once alive. When the burning is completed only carbon is left. Carbon is an element represented by the symbol C. The paper, leaves, and sugar turned black—carbon. If carbon is heated to a very high temperature, it can form the gas carbon dioxide. Topsoil is darker than subsoil, because it contains rotten plants and animals, which contain carbon. The graphite in your pencil is carbon.

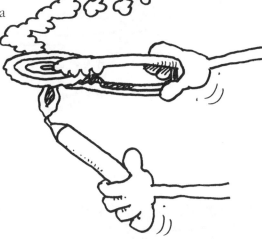

126 Changing Shape

Find out which materials can easily change shape.

Materials
- pieces of different household and garden materials (newspaper, wood, baking paper, foil, metal, fabrics, twigs, sand, rocks, bone, clay, sheep's wool, plastic, paper, cardboard, leaves, feathers etc.)

STEPS

1. Test each material to see if it can squash, bend, twist, or stretch.
2. Sort the materials into two groups—those that can easily change shape, and those that can't. Can you change them back to their original shape?

Did You Know?
The shape of some materials is easily changed. For example, an elastic band needs to stretch easily and change back to its original form to do its job. Other materials, such as brick, are very hard to change, so they give strength to a wall.

127 Colorful Sugar

Materials
- 4 teaspoons sugar
- 20 teaspoons water
- food dye
- bowl
- sunny spot

Create colorful sugar crystals.

STEPS

1. Stir the sugar into the water until it dissolves (disappears).
2. Add a few drops of food dye.
3. Leave the bowl in a sunny spot for a few days. What happens?

"I feel like we've been out here for days in this sun! At this rate we're going to turn into sugar crystals!"

"I think that's the idea!"

Did You Know?
With the sun's heat, the water will evaporate from the bowl, leaving the sugar and dye behind.

128 Conduction

Materials
- hot water
- drinking glass
- ceramic mug
- polystyrene cup

Find out which material is a better conductor of heat.

STEPS

1. Fill the glass, the mug, and the cup with the hot water.
2. Gently place your hand around the outside of each container, one at a time.
3. Which feels hottest? Which feels coolest?

Did You Know?
Some materials let heat through more easily than others. These are called good "conductors" of heat. The heat travels or "conducts" through the material. The glass should have felt the hottest, because it is the best conductor of heat. The polystyrene should have felt the coolest, because it is a poor conductor of heat. This is why hot drinks are often served in polystyrene cups, to keep the heat in the drink for longer.

OUCH!

UMMM...

AAAH THAT'S BETTER!

129 Cooling Down

Find out what happens to some different materials when they are cooled.

Materials
- different household materials (water, vinegar, bread, rice, butter etc.)
- containers
- freezer

STEPS

1. Place each material into a container. Draw a picture and describe its feel.
2. Place the containers in the freezer overnight.
3. Check the materials the next day—what are they like now? Draw a second picture and describe what they feel like.

I'm squashing my important scientific experiments in the freezer ... between the frozen peas and the hot dogs. Please don't use them for dinner.

Did You Know?

Cooling materials can change them. For example, some liquids will have changed into a solid, such as water into ice. Some materials may not have changed much at all, such as the rice. We can cool foods to keep them fresh for longer.

---

130 Corny Goo

Make a goo with strange habits.

Materials
- water
- 2 tablespoons cornstarch
- bowl
- spoon

STEPS

1. Put two tablespoons of cornstarch into the bowl.
2. Add a tablespoon of water to the cornstarch, stirring well with the spoon. Keep adding water a few drops at a time until the goo is thick and creamy.
3. Pick up the goo and roll it between your fingers. Stop rolling—what happens?

Did You Know?

When you roll the goo, it feels dry and hard, like a solid. When you stop rolling, it slowly spreads over your fingers, like a liquid. Cornstarch particles float in water. When you roll the cornstarch and water, the particles are forced together. When you stop rolling, the cornstarch and water separate again. Corny goo behaves much like quicksand!

131 Green Slime

Make green slime.

STEPS

1. In a container, mix together one tablespoon of glue, one tablespoon of water and one drop of green food dye.

2. In a separate container, dissolve one teaspoon of borax powder in one tablespoon of water. Borax powder is poisonous—wash your hands after touching it or your slime!

3. Pour the borax solution into your glue mixture. Mix with your fingers—a "slime" should form instantly!

4. Store in an airtight container.

> I don't like the way that green slime is behaving at all!
>
> Something that gooey shouldn't be let out.

Materials
- wood glue
- borax powder (laundry section in supermarket)
- green food dye
- water

Did You Know?

The glue and borax mix together to make a new chemical—the slime! The borax stops the glue flowing like a liquid. The slime is very elastic, so it can even bounce if you roll it into a ball!

---

132 Fast Rust

Make steel rust quickly.

STEPS

1. Place the steel wool into the jar then cover it with water.

2. Pour in a dash of vinegar and a dash of bleach.

3. Wait for a few hours, and watch the steel go rusty!

Materials
- steel wool (not the soapy kind)
- jar
- water
- vinegar
- bleach

Did You Know?

Rust forms when iron is combined with oxygen and water. The vinegar strips any protective coating off the steel, and oxygen in the bleach combines with the iron in the steel. This makes the wet steel go rusty very quickly. If you wrap the steel around the bulb of a thermometer, you should be able to see the temperature rise! This is because this chemical reaction gives off heat energy.

133 Materials and Their Uses

Choose the correct materials for the job.

STEPS

1. Walk around the house and yard looking for all the things made of wood. Record some of the uses of wood, for example, wood is used for fences, spoons, chairs and tables etc.

2. Repeat the survey for plastic, metal, and glass.

3. Which do you think is the most useful material to people? Why?

Materials
- house
- yard
- paper
- pencil

Did You Know?

Choosing the right materials for different uses is very important. For example, a glass chair or a plastic pan would not be very easy to use! New materials are being invented all the time to suit different uses, for example, polar fleece for light, yet warm, clothing.

---

134 Melt or Burn?

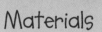

See what happens when you heat different solids.

STEPS

1. Ask an adult to help you light the candle.

2. Hold a solid with tongs and heat it over the flame for about a minute.

3. Observe carefully what happens to each solid. Does it change? Does it melt or burn? If it burns is anything left when it stops burning?

4. Drop the solid into the cold water. Draw a picture of what happened to the solid.

5. Repeat for all the solids. Do all substances change the same way when they are heated? Which substances change when they are hot but go back to their original form when they cool again? Which substances change permanently?

Materials
- different household solids (ice, plastic, metal, yarn, leaf, paper, cardboard, rock)
- lit candle
- container of water
- tongs with insulated handles

Did You Know?

Different substances change in different ways when you heat them. Some you can change back to their original form (ice into water), and these are called reversible changes. Irreversible changes are when you can't reverse the change, like when paper burns into ash and smoke.

135 Preserving Food

Compare different ways of stopping bread from going moldy.

Materials
- 4 pieces of bread
- 4 jars with lids
- vinegar
- water
- salt

STEPS

1. Place a piece of bread into each jar.
2. Add water to one jar so it just covers the bread.
3. Add vinegar to the next jar, so it just covers the bread.
4. Dissolve a few teaspoons of salt in some water. Add this to a jar, just covering the bread.
5. Leave the fourth piece of bread untouched.
6. Leave the jars for several days. Each day, check if any mold has grown.

I think the piece of bread in this jar will walk away on its own when I take the lid off.

Did You Know?

Foods contain yeasts and bacteria, which after some time can grow and make the food go moldy and unhealthy to eat. Vinegar and salt kill most of these organisms, so pieces of bread soaked in these jars should go moldy last, or not at all. Before refrigerators were invented, using salt was an important way to preserve foods.

136 The Floating Egg

Find out which liquids an egg will float in.

Materials
- 4 glasses of water
- salt
- sugar
- flour
- fresh egg

STEPS

1. Fill each glass three-quarters full with water.
2. Stir a few tablespoons of salt into one glass of water, until it dissolves.
3. Stir the same amount of sugar into the second glass of water.
4. Stir the same amount of flour into the third glass of water. Leave the fourth glass of water plain.
5. Guess which glass of liquid the egg will float in. Now try them all!

Did You Know?

Density is how tightly the matter of a mixture is packed together. For example, an egg is more dense than plain water, so the egg sinks. Salt water, however, is more dense than an egg, and so the egg floats! Are you more or less dense than sea water? Note: If the egg is stale it will float in water because gas forms inside the egg when the egg is going bad. You can use this trick to check the freshness of an egg.

137 Save Our Chemicals!

Look after our environment by recycling chemicals.

STEPS

1. Search the house and yard, and a local park or street (with the permission of an adult) for chemicals you can recycle. For example, collect empty cans and old newspapers.

2. Collect all the paper in one plastic bag, cans in another bag, glass bottles in another. Leave them for the recycling company to pick up!

Note: Some city councils provide residents with special bins to use when disposing of recyclable waste. If your family has one, see what you can recycle.

Materials
- house
- yard
- park
- streets
- plastic bags
- gardening gloves

Did You Know?

A lot of energy goes into making new chemicals, or getting them out of the Earth. We can recycle many chemicals, such as glass, paper, and some plastics, and make them into new objects. This means that we can save energy and limit the damage done to our environment.

---

138 Sorting Materials

Describe and sort materials.

STEPS

1. Look at each material closely. Draw a picture of it.

2. Around the picture, write adjectives to describe the material. Use words such as hard, soft, shiny, dull, bendy, etc.

3. Are there any groups you could sort the materials into, for example, heavy and light? How many different ways can you sort your objects?

Materials
- a collection of different materials (spoons, keys, wooden objects, fabrics)
- paper
- pencils

Did You Know?

In science we often sort things into groups, depending on their characteristics. For example, animals can be divided into mammals, reptiles, birds, and insects. Chemicals can be sorted into those that dissolve in water and those that won't.

139 Stretchy Stockings

Discover which pair of tights is the most stretchy.

STEPS

1. Hang a pair of tights up high on the washing line.
2. Place the weight into one "foot." With the ruler, measure how much the tights stretched.
3. Repeat your test for the other pairs of tights. Draw a bar graph of the different lengths the tights stretched.

Note: Don't choose your mother's best stockings for this experiment!

Has anybody seen my good pair of tights that I'm wearing out to dinner and the movies tonight?

Materials
- different pairs of tights
- a weight, such as a rock
- ruler

Did You Know?

Before the invention of nylon, stockings were made from wool, silk, and cotton. The first nylon stockings went on sale in 1940. At first, they were made to the exact shape of the leg, because they could not stretch. In 1959 Lycra was invented, which could stretch up to seven times its original length without breaking!

---

140 What Is It?

Identify materials using your senses of touch, hearing, and smell.

STEPS

1. Ask a friend to place different objects into the bag for you—don't look!
2. Using your senses of touch, hearing, and smell, pick up each object in the bag and try to guess what it is.
3. Give yourself a point for each one you guess correctly. Swap—this time you place objects in the bag for a friend to guess! Which sense was the most useful in this activity?

This experiment is sort of like a scientific lucky dip! Hope I don't pick anything spiky!

Materials
- a collection of different objects (spoons, keys, wooden objects, papers, fabrics)
- large bag

Did You Know?

We often use our senses to work out what is in the world around us. For some people, who are blind or deaf, this process becomes much more difficult. In this activity, the sense of touch was probably the most useful.

141 Wrinkly Apple

Create your own mummified apple face.

Materials
- 1 apple
- 1 ice cream stick
- 1 plastic bag
- ¼ cup salt
- ½ cup sodium carbonate (powder bleach)
- ½ cup baking soda

STEPS

1. Mix the salt, sodium carbonate, and baking soda together in the bag.
2. Cut a face into the apple using the ice cream stick. Push the stick into the top of your apple so it makes a handle.
3. Put the apple into the mixture in the bag, so it is covered.
4. Leave the bag open, in a warm place. Watch what happens to the apple!

Hard to tell whether this is an apple or a wrinkly prune! But the experiment says it's an apple ... so we'll go with that!

Did You Know?
The powders take all the moisture out of the apple, and make it difficult for bacteria to grow. Without the water and bacteria, the apple cannot decay, so it just shrivels and dries up. **Do not eat this apple!**

142 Brown Apples

You can stop a cut apple turning brown.

Materials
- apple
- lemon juice
- knife

STEPS

1. Cut an apple in half.
2. Spread lemon juice over one cut half, and leave the other half untouched.
3. Leave both halves out in the air. Check every 15 minutes to notice any changes.

Did You Know?
Air contains a gas called oxygen. Oxygen reacts with some foods, like apples, to make it go brown. The foods "oxidize." Some chemicals, such as lemon juice, slow down this reaction. This tip can be used when making fruit salads to keep the fruit looking nice! Try this experiment with other fruits.

143 Rubbery Egg

Can you make an eggshell go soft?

Materials
- 1 egg
- drinking glass
- vinegar

STEPS

1. Gently place the egg into the glass.
2. Pour vinegar over the egg to completely cover it.
3. Wait several days. Take the egg out of the glass and feel the shell.

Did You Know?

The vinegar reacts with the calcium in the eggshell, dissolving it. This makes the shell feel rubbery. This shows the importance of calcium to make the shell strong, just like the calcium in our bones. Keep drinking that milk!

144 Milky Plastic

Make a milky plastic.

Materials
- glass full-cream milk
- vinegar
- eye dropper

STEPS

1. Ask an adult to help you warm up the milk by microwaving it for a minute or by placing it in a bowl of hot water.
2. Slowly squirt the vinegar into the warm milk and stir.
3. Make sure the mixture is not too hot, then slowly pour the milk out onto your hand (over the sink!), "catching" the plastic in your fingers!

Did You Know?

Milk contains a chemical called casein. Casein can be separated from the rest of the milk using the vinegar. This is a type of plastic, which is a chemical made of long chains of many small parts (atoms) joined together.

145 Acid or Base?

Which chemicals are acids and which are bases?

STEPS

1. Chop up the cabbage leaves into small pieces. Ask for help to boil some water and cover the pieces then let them soak for half an hour. Separate the cooled "cabbage juice" from the leaves.

2. Pour some of each chemical (vinegar, lemon juice, baking soda, and laundry detergent) into a separate jar.

3. Add a dash of your cabbage juice to each chemical.

4. If the mixture turns pink, the chemical you tested is an acid. If the mixture turns blue/green, the chemical is a base.

Materials
- red cabbage leaves
- boiling water
- vinegar
- lemon juice or lemonade
- baking soda
- laundry detergent

Did You Know?

Chemicals can be acids or bases. The "cabbage juice" is called an indicator. It can show you whether a chemical is an acid or a base by changing its color. Test some other chemicals around the house to see if they are acids or bases—try toothpaste or orange juice!

146 Clean Cleaner

Compare the cleaning action of vinegar and a supermarket cleaner.

STEPS

1. Find a dirty mirror or window.

2. Scrunch up a sheet of newspaper and pour some vinegar on it. Scrub half of the mirror or window.

3. Spray some cleaning product onto the mirror or window. Using the cleaning cloth, rub the other half of the mirror or window.

4. Which half of the glass is cleaner? Is there much of a difference? Which way is more environmentally friendly?

Materials
- vinegar
- cleaning product for mirrors and windows
- newspaper
- a cleaning cloth

Ahh!
Just beautiful!
Absolutely beautiful ...
The clean mirror I mean.
Not me.

Did You Know?

Many cleaning products contain toxic chemicals that pollute our waterways. Vinegar is a good cleaner and is non-toxic. A lot of energy goes into making cleaning cloths. Recycling newspaper means you don't need to buy cleaning cloths!

147 Clean Money

Clean some coins using acid.

This is my hard-earned pocket money we're experimenting on here. Let's just give it a shine up ... not dissolve it away.

Materials
- glass of cola drink
- dirty coins

STEPS

1. Drop the dirty coins into the glass of cola drink.
2. Check the coins after a day or two. What happened?

Did You Know?

Cola drinks contain food acids. The acids react with the dirt on the coins, and so "clean" them.

---

148 Disappearing Act

Find some materials that can dissolve in water.

STEPS

1. Fill the glasses three-quarters full with warm water.
2. Place two teaspoons of salt into one glass. Stir quickly and count until the salt has disappeared.
3. Place two teaspoons of sugar into another glass. Stir quickly and count until the sugar has disappeared.
4. Repeat with two teaspoons of sand in the third glass. What happens?

Yuck! This tastes like I'm drinking the ocean! This must be the salty one!

Materials
- warm water
- 3 glasses
- salt
- sugar
- sand
- spoons

Did You Know?

Some materials, such as sugar and salt, easily dissolve in water. They break down until we can't see them anymore, but if we tasted the water, we would notice they were still there. Some materials, such as sand, do not dissolve in water and so will never "disappear." Imagine how much salt is dissolved in sea water!

149 Crystal Star

Make your own crystal star.

STEPS

1. Cut a pipe cleaner into four pieces, and twist the lengths together to form a star shape.
2. Tie a length of string to one "arm" of the star. Tie the other end around the ice cream stick.
3. Ask an adult to help you dissolve the borax powder in boiling water, about three tablespoons per cup of water. Half fill the jar. Add a few drops of food dye if you like. Borax powder is poisonous—wash your hands after touching it.
4. Place the ice cream stick across the top of the jar, so your star hangs into the borax water. Wait a few days for your star to grow!

Materials
- borax powder (laundry section in supermarket)
- hot water
- jar
- ice cream stick
- cotton string
- pipe cleaner
- food dye
- scissors

Did You Know?
The borax powder dissolves in the water. When the water evaporates, the borax is left behind, and attaches to the pipe cleaner "star" as tiny crystals.

150 Crystals Everywhere

Watch stars appear when tiny crystals grow.

STEPS

1. Cut a star shape out of the cardboard, so you are left with a stencil. Throw out the star.
2. Dissolve the Epsom salts in half a cup of hot water. Keep adding salt until no more will dissolve.
3. Dip the sponge into the salt water. Placing the stencil over the black paper, rub the sponge over the star shape, onto the black cardboard.
4. Carefully lift the stencil to another area on the paper. "Paint" more star shapes with your salt water until you run out of room on the black paper.
5. Let your paper dry. The crystal stars will appear!

Materials
- large sheet of black cardboard
- scissors
- ½ cup hot water
- Epsom salts (laundry section in supermarket)
- small sponge

Did You Know?
The Epsom salts dissolve in the hot water. When you use it to paint on the black paper, the water evaporates, and the Epsom salts are left behind, forming small crystals on the paper.

151 Climbing Colors

Find the hidden colors inside ink.

Materials
- different colored markers (water-based, not permanent)
- coffee filter paper or paper towel
- drinking glass
- water
- scissors

STEPS

1. Cut some strips of dry filter paper. Each one should be about 1 in (2.5 cm) wide and long enough to reach the bottom of the glass.
2. Draw a dot with a marker, about 1 in (2.5 cm) from the bottom of one strip.
3. Place the strip into ½ in (1 cm) of water in the glass, leaning the strip against the edge of the glass. Make sure the water level is below the dot!
4. The water should rise up the paper, past the dot, and carry the ink upward. The ink will separate into its different colors.
5. Repeat with the other strips, with different colored dots on each strip.

Did You Know?

Many inks are actually mixtures of different colors. As the water carries the ink up through the paper, these colors separate because some move farther and faster than others. This way, you can discover which colors are used to make up the ink.

152 Gas to Liquid

See the water that exists in air.

Materials
- glass jar with lid
- ice cubes
- salt
- tissue

STEPS

1. Fill the jar with ice cubes and add two tablespoons of salt. Screw on the lid, then shake!
2. Slowly watch water droplets appear on the outside of the jar. Wrap the tissue around the jar, then take it off to see how wet it is!

Did You Know?

The salted ice quickly makes the glass sides of the jar very cold. The water that exists in the air as a gas cools down and changes into a liquid when it hits the cold sides of the jar. This process is called condensation (which is the opposite to evaporation). This allows you to see the water that is usually invisible in the air! You can collect the water using the tissue.

153 Hard and Soft Water

What is the difference between "hard" and "soft" water?

STEPS

1. Place two cups of water into each bottle. Add two teaspoons of Epsom salts to one of the bottles. Screw the lids on and shake.
2. Add a few drops of dishwashing liquid to both bottles. Replace the lids and shake.
3. What do you notice?

Materials
- 2 clean empty soda bottles with lids
- Epsom salts (laundry section in supermarket)
- dishwashing liquid

Did You Know?

The bottle with the Epsom salts should have fewer bubbles than the plain water. This is because you have made the water "hard." Water in some areas is hard because it has minerals dissolved in it. These minerals interfere with the action of detergents. Chemicals can be added to hard water to make it "soft" again, so that detergents can do their work.

---

154 Homemade Glue

Make a non-toxic, environmentally friendly glue.

Materials
- flour
- water
- jar with lid
- spoon
- brush

STEPS

1. Mix one cup flour with half a cup of water together in the jar, stirring well. This becomes the glue!
2. Use your brush to glue newspaper pages together into shapes. Let them dry. What happens?

Did You Know?

This is a chemical reaction, and the paste sets hard when it dries. After your newspaper shapes have dried, you can even paint them different colors!

I have absolutely no idea what I'm making... but at least it will be well glued!

155 Invisible Ink

Write an invisible message and watch it reappear.

Materials
- lemon juice (bottled is fine)
- a cotton swab
- a piece of white writing paper
- clothes iron

STEPS

1. Dip the cotton swab into the lemon juice, and use this "pen" to write an invisible message or picture on the paper.
2. Wait for your "ink" to air-dry and completely disappear.
3. Ask an adult to help you iron over the dry paper. Watch your message reveal itself!

Did You Know?

The heat changes the lemon juice into a new chemical. This chemical is brown and so your message can be seen on the white paper. Eventually, the paper would also turn brown and burn, but the lemon juice changes more quickly. Try using other acids such as vinegar as your ink!

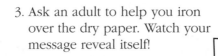

156 Sweaty Eggplants

Watch an eggplant "sweat."

Materials
- 2 slices of eggplant
- 2 teaspoons of salt

STEPS

1. Ask an adult to help you cut two slices off an eggplant.
2. Sprinkle two teaspoons of salt over one of the slices, and leave the other untouched.
3. After half an hour, look closely at both slices. The salted slice will appear "sweaty," with drops of water coming out of it!

Did You Know?

An eggplant is a plant, so water can flow in or out of its tiny cells. When you sprinkle salt onto the eggplant slice, there is more salt in the surroundings than inside the plant, so water leaves the cells. This makes the eggplant appear to "sweat." This process is used in cooking to take the bitterness out of the eggplant.

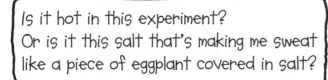

157 Melting Ice

Find out which spot in the house or yard is warmest.

Materials
- 5 containers
- 10 ice cubes

STEPS

1. Place two ice cubes in each container.
2. Place the five containers in different spots around the house and yard. Guess which will melt first, and which last.
3. Check to see which ice melts first, second, third, fourth, and fifth. Why do you think this happened?

Guess which ice cube spent ten minutes beside the heater and which one didn't.

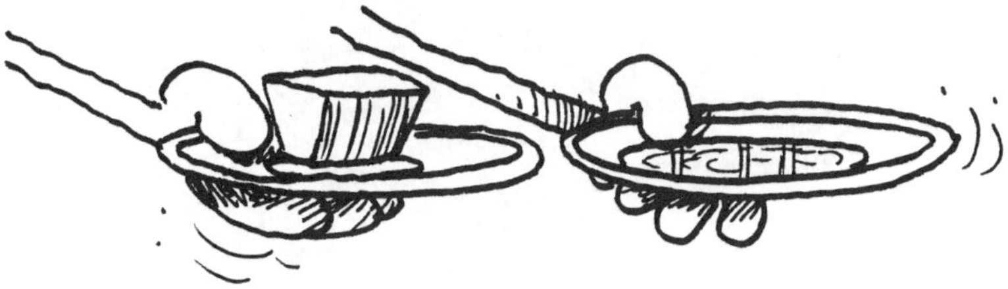

Did You Know?

Placing the container in a sunny place, or close to a light bulb or a heater, would have melted the ice quickly. Dark and cool places, such as inside a cabinet, would probably keep the ice cold (and frozen) longer.

---

158 Salty Ice

Melt an ice cube quickly.

Materials
- 2 ice cubes
- salt
- 2 bowls

STEPS

1. Place each ice cube into a separate bowl.
2. Sprinkle a teaspoon of salt onto one of the ice cubes.
3. Watch the ice cubes melt. Which one wins the melting race?

Did You Know?

Salt makes ice cubes melt faster. Plain water freezes at 32°F (0°C). Salt lowers the freezing temperature of water, so the ice cube in salt would have to be made much colder than 32°F (0°C) to stay frozen. At room temperature this is not possible, so the ice has to melt.

159 Baked Ice Cream

Bake ice cream in your oven without it melting.

STEPS

1. Ask an adult to heat the oven to 500°F (260°C).
2. Place the foil on top of the baking sheet.
3. Beat the egg whites with the sugar until you have glossy peaks.
4. Place the biscuit on the foil, and top with the ice cream. Spread the egg white all over the ice cream, to cover it all.
5. Place the baking sheet in the oven, near the bottom, for about five minutes. When the egg white has browned slightly, remove and eat!

Materials
- 3 egg whites
- ½ cup sugar
- a big, thick biscuit
- 1 cup ice cream
- baking sheet
- foil
- oven

Did You Know?
When you beat the egg whites, a lot of tiny air bubbles were made and trapped in the foam. These air bubbles protected the ice cream in the oven, slowing the hot air getting to the ice cream, so that it did not melt! Yum!

160 Squishy Ice Cream

Make your own ice cream.

STEPS

1. Mix the milk, sugar, and vanilla in the small bag, seal, and shake!
2. Mix the ice and salt in the bigger bag.
3. Put the small bag inside the big bag. Squish them together for 10 minutes or so, with your fingers. The longer you knead, the creamier the ice cream!
4. Eat!

I'm sure having ten frozen fingers will be worth it for extra creamy ice cream in this experiment!

Materials
- ½ cup full-cream milk
- 1 tablespoon sugar
- 1 teaspoon vanilla essence
- 1 large zip-lock bag
- 1 small zip-lock bag
- 2 cups crushed ice
- 6 tablespoons of salt

Did You Know?
The salt makes the ice even colder, and so freezes the milk mixture. Because you keep squishing, the mixture becomes creamy!

161 Peppery Skin

Show that water has an invisible "skin."

STEPS
1. Fill the bowl with water.
2. Sprinkle pepper all over the surface of the water.
3. Gently add a drop of detergent to the middle of the bowl. What happens?

Materials
- large, flat bowl
- water
- pepper
- dishwashing liquid

Did You Know?
You should have seen the surface of pepper split, or fracture, when you dropped the detergent in. This is because detergent breaks up the invisible "skin" of water, and the pepper allows you to see this happening.

162 Soap Boats

Make a boat move across water using soap.

STEPS
1. Place the plastic tie or cardboard boat onto the water.
2. Carefully place a few drops of dishwashing liquid into the "V" shape of the boat.
3. Watch your boat move forward across the water!

Materials
- one plastic bread-bag tie, or a piece of cardboard cut into a boat shape, with a "V" shape cut into one edge (see picture to the left)
- large container of water
- dishwashing liquid or small piece of soap

Did You Know?
The dishwashing liquid mixes into the water, and weakens the attraction between the water and the back of the boat. The pull of the water on the front of the boat is now stronger, so moves the boat forward. Try this experiment by wedging a small piece of hand soap into the "V."

163 Swirly Patterns

Make swirly patterns in milk.

STEPS

1. Fill the bowl or plate with milk, about 1 in (2.5 cm) deep.
2. Add a few drops of different food dyes on top of the milk, around the edges of the plate or bowl, keeping the dyes separate. Do not mix them into the milk!
3. Add a few drops of dishwashing liquid in the middle of the bowl.
4. Watch the swirly patterns form!

Materials
- flat bowl or deep plate
- dishwashing liquid
- different food dyes
- milk

Did You Know?

The detergent changes the surface of the milk, making the water in the milk flow more easily. This causes a swirling motion, easily seen by the movement of the food dye. Try this activity with low-fat milk to see whether this makes any difference!

---

164 Wax Factor

Can you make a new candle out of bits and pieces of old ones?

STEPS

1. Put the candles and wax crayons in the pan.
2. Ask an adult to help you melt them slowly over a low heat. Stir gently to swirl the mix together and make a pattern with the colors.
3. While the wax is melting (make sure you keep an eye on it because you just want to melt the wax, not cook it), make a small hole in the bottom of the polystyrene cup with a skewer.
4. Thread the string through the hole; tie a knot underneath. The string should be long enough for you to be able to hang your candle out to dry.
5. Ask an adult to help you pour the wax into the paper cup. Be careful! The melted wax is very hot and will burn if you get it on your fingers.
6. Hang it up by its long string to dry.
7. When the wax has hardened, cut off the string, leaving enough at the top for a wick.

Note: before you light your new candle it is important to remove the polystyrene cup.

Materials
- pieces of used white candles
- used, colored wax crayons
- pan
- string
- spoon
- skewer
- heat-resistant, disposable polystyrene cup

Did You Know?

Wax can change from a solid to a liquid when it is heated. It becomes a solid again when it cools.

165 Candy Dissolving

How long can you make candy last?

STEPS

1. Place one candy into your mouth. Time how long it takes to dissolve, without using your tongue or your teeth to help!

2. Place the second candy into your mouth. Time how long it takes to dissolve, using only your tongue.

3. Place the third candy into your mouth. Time how long it takes to dissolve, using both your tongue and your teeth.

4. Compare the three times taken. What do you notice?

Materials
- 3 pieces of hard candy, about the same size
- timer or clock

Did You Know?
Dissolving is easier if the pieces are smaller, and if you can "Stir." So the candy should have dissolved fastest when you could use your tongue and teeth to help!

---

166 Tilted Bottle

Observe what happens to the water level in a tilted bottle.

STEPS

1. Half fill the bottle with water and screw the lid on. Draw the bottle and the water level.

2. Tilt the bottle a little on its side. Draw it again, noting the water level.

3. Tilt the bottle farther and draw it and the water level again.

4. Lie the bottle flat on the table. Draw it and the water level again. What did you notice?

Materials
- a clear, plastic bottle with lid
- water
- paper
- pencil

Did You Know?
The water level always stays flat, or horizontal. It stays parallel with the ground because gravity pulls it down equally on all sides.

167 Volume

Find out how much water is moved by different weights.

STEPS

1. Half fill each of the glasses with water, to the same level.
2. Completely fill one jar with sand and fill the other jar only half full. Screw on the lids.
3. Sink the half-full jar into one glass of water. How much does the water rise?
4. Sink the full jar into the second glass. How much did the water rise this time?

Materials
- 2 same-sized glasses
- 2 same-sized jars with lids (smaller than the glasses)
- sand
- water

Did You Know?
When something sinks, it moves some water aside. In a glass, the water must move up. Because the full jar of sand is heavier, it needs to move aside more water. This is why the water will move up higher in the glass.

168 Will It Mix?

Not all liquids will mix with water.

STEPS

1. Add a few tablespoons of one of the liquids to the jar of water. Mix well.
2. Look closely at the mixture. Has the liquid mixed in with the water, or does it float on top or settle on the bottom?
3. Rinse the jar in soapy water, and test all the liquids. Do they all mix with water?

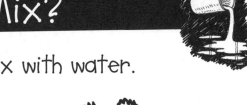

Materials
- different household liquids (methylated spirits, juice, cooking oil, sunscreen, ink, detergent, milk, vinegar, engine oil etc.)
- jar of water
- stirrers
- soapy water

Did You Know?
Not all liquids can mix with water. For example, oil and water do not mix. The oil floats on the water.

169 The Big Freeze

Find out how quickly water freezes.

Materials
- 2 ice cube trays
- freezer
- warm water
- cold water

STEPS

1. Fill one ice cube tray with cold water, and the other with warm water.
2. Place them both in a freezer. Which will freeze first?
3. Every 15 minutes, check the ice cubes. What happens?

Let's just see how those warm water ice cubes are freezing!

Did You Know?

The warm water will take longer to freeze, because it takes more energy to turn warm water into a solid than cold water. This is because in warm water the particles are moving faster around each other than in cold water, and so it takes more energy to slow them down into a solid.

---

170 The Big Ice

Does water expand or shrink when it turns into ice?

Materials
- glass of water
- ice cube

STEPS

1. Fill the glass with water, almost up to the rim.
2. Carefully place the ice cube on top of the water.
3. Watch as the ice cube melts. Have a guess whether the water will overflow out of the glass!

Did You Know?

Ice takes up more space than liquid water. This is why, when the ice cube melts, the water should not overflow. The ice cube will melt into liquid water, which will take up less space than the original ice cube occupied.

171 Is That Egg Hard-boiled?

Can you find out if an egg is raw or hard-boiled without breaking the shell?

STEPS

1. Spin the egg on its side and hold it for a moment.
2. Let the egg go.
3. If it keeps spinning it's the raw egg, and if it stops, it's hard boiled.

Did You Know?

The raw egg keeps spinning because it still has liquid inside. When you hold the egg the liquid keeps turning. When you release the egg, the spinning liquid inside keeps the egg turning. This is useful to know if you forget which egg you boiled for your lunch!

Materials
- Hard-boiled egg
- Raw egg
- Smooth surface (that the eggs can't roll off)

---

172 Blowing Bubbles

Find out which detergent is best for blowing bubbles.

STEPS

1. Add a few tablespoons of each detergent to a different jar of water. Mix well. Leave for a day if possible.
2. Dip one end of the straw into each jar, and try blowing bubbles. Which detergent works best?
3. Dip the wire loop into each jar, and try blowing bubbles. Does it work better than the straw?
4. How long do your bubbles last before they pop? Describe and draw the bubbles you blow!
5. If your hands are wet and soapy, sometimes you can catch the bubbles before they "pop."

Materials
- different household detergents (shampoo, dishwashing liquid, bubble bath etc.)
- jars of water
- drinking straws
- wire loops (florist wire works well)

Did You Know?

A bubble is actually a thin "skin" of detergent, filled with air. The bubble pops if: the skin is stretched too thin; it hits something so the skin breaks; or the air inside expands too much.

173 Bubbly Drink

Make your own bubbly fruit drink.

STEPS

1. Squeeze the orange juice into the glass.
2. Add the same amount of water to the glass.
3. Stir in a teaspoon of baking soda.
4. Take a sip to taste the bubbles! Add a little sugar to make it sweeter, if you like.

Materials
- orange
- water
- baking soda
- glass
- sugar (optional)

Did You Know?

The bubbles are made from the reaction between the acid in the orange and the baking soda. These bubbles are actually a gas, just like in soda..

---

174 Diving Raisins

Make raisins dive up and down without touching them.

STEPS

1. Place the baking soda into the glass.
2. Slowly pour the vinegar into the glass, taking care it does not overflow!
3. Drop the raisins into the glass, and watch them bounce up and down!

Materials
- 10 raisins
- 1 tall glass
- 2 tablespoons of baking soda
- white vinegar

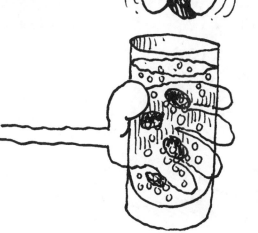

Did You Know?

The baking soda and vinegar mix together to make a gas called carbon dioxide. The bubbles of gas attach to the raisins and carry them up to the surface. At the surface the bubbles pop, which sends the raisin diving down to the bottom again. Does this experiment work in a glass of fizzy lemonade? The bubbles in soda are also carbon dioxide gas.

175 Fire Extinguisher

Put out a candle flame (not using your breath).

Materials
- a lit candle
- empty film canister
- baking soda
- vinegar

STEPS

1. Ask an adult to help you light the candle.
2. Place a teaspoon of baking soda into the film canister.
3. Pour a little vinegar into the canister, and quickly put the lid on.
4. Shake the canister, take the lid off, and quickly point the opening of the canister just above the candle flame. Watch the flame suddenly go out!

Did You Know?

The baking soda and vinegar mix together and make a gas called carbon dioxide. This gas, which is heavier than air, pours out of the canister and down over the flame, stopping oxygen in the air from fueling the fire.

176 Lights Out

Another way to make a candle go out without blowing it.

Materials
- 1 lit candle
- a glass
- a metal lid

STEPS

1. Ask an adult to help you gently place a candle into a glass and light it. The candle needs to be shorter than the glass!
2. Carefully place a metal lid on top of the glass that completely covers the opening.
3. Watch the candle go out after a minute or so.

Did You Know?

Fire needs fuel and oxygen to burn. The wax of the candle is the fuel, and the oxygen comes from the air. When you place the lid on top of the glass, you block the oxygen getting to the flame, and the fire will go out. This is the reason heaping sand over a campfire will make it go out by suffocating the fire.

177 Fizzy Sherbet

Make your own delicious fizzy sherbet.

STEPS

1. In a bowl, mix the icing sugar, acid, and baking soda together. Add the jelly crystals.
2. Eat!

Did You Know?

The acid makes the icing sugar taste tangy. When the baking soda is added, it reacts with the acid to make bubbles of carbon dioxide gas, which makes the sherbet fizzy on your tongue! Be careful—if you eat too much, you will burp a lot from all that gas!

BURP!

Whoops! A little too much of this scientific sherbet perhaps!

Materials
- 20 teaspoons icing sugar
- 1 teaspoon citric or tartaric acid
- 1 teaspoon baking soda
- 1 teaspoon jelly crystals

178 Green to Red

Watch a tomato ripen.

STEPS

1. Place one tomato in each paper bag.
2. Add the banana to one of the bags, and close the openings of the bags.
3. Place the bags in a cool place.
4. Every day, check the tomatoes. After a few days, the tomato in the bag with the banana should turn red first.

Did You Know?

Ethylene is a natural gas that ripens fruit. Without ethylene some fruits, such as bananas, would never ripen. The banana's ethylene gas helps to ripen the tomato in the bag. The tomato without the banana will also make its own ethylene, it just won't ripen as quickly. Ethylene also wilts flowers, so keep your bananas away from your fresh-cut flowers.

Materials
- 2 green tomatoes
- 1 banana
- 2 paper bags

Hmmm ... Cheese and tomato sandwiches for lunch tomorrow?

179 Smell That Gas

How fast does a gas travel through air?

Materials
- perfume or air freshener
- large room

STEPS

1. Spray the perfume or air freshener in one corner of the room.
2. Run over to the other corner of the room and count how long before you can smell the perfume.

I don't know why I'm running, well hopping in my case, to the other side of the room to see how long it takes for the air freshener to reach me ... I don't have a nose to smell it!

Did You Know?

The perfume is a liquid, but when we spray it, it evaporates into a gas. This gas spreads out and travels through the gases of the air. When we breathe in air, the smell is noticed in our nose. Because many gases are invisible and poisonous, they can be dangerous. This is why natural gas has a smell added to it, so we know when it is in the air around us.

---

180 Tall or Short?

How fast does evaporation occur in different containers?

Materials
- tall, narrow container
- wide, shallow container
- water
- plastic ruler
- sunny spot

STEPS

1. Pour the same amount of water into both containers. Measure the depth of each.
2. Leave the bowls in a sunny spot. Every hour, measure the depth of each.
3. Which liquid goes down fastest? After a few days, which container is dry first?

Did You Know?

Liquids can evaporate, or change into a gas, when they are heated. The water in the wide, shallow container should evaporate first, because there is more surface area where it can change into a gas.

181 Pangaea: The Ancient Continent

Investigate the shape of the continents and the history of Earth.

Materials
- a photocopy of a map of the world
- large sheet of paper, the same size as your map
- scissors
- glue

STEPS

1. Cut the seven continents out from your map of the world.
2. Spread the large sheet of paper on a table.
3. Take the continents you have cut out and place them on the paper. Play around with the continents and see how you can get them to fit together. Do any of them fit together like the pieces of a jigsaw?
4. When you have found some pieces that match, glue them next to each other on your paper. Glue the other continents around the outside. Now you have Pangaea.

Did You Know?

Because the continents are shaped the way they are, scientists think that they were once joined as one super-continent. This means that fossils of ancestors of animals that live in only one place today can be found in places all over the world.

182 Making Sandstone

Make your very own piece of sandstone.

STEPS

1. Half fill a small paper cup with sand.
2. Slowly add the cementing solution until it completely covers the sand.
3. Now you have to let your mixture set. Make sure you place the cup in a warm place (i.e. a kitchen cabinet). Keep it there overnight.
4. In the morning, remove the dry mixture from the cup. It may still be a little wet, but should still be dry enough to hold its shape. Place the mixture on a paper towel for a farther two days, or until it is completely dry.
5. Congratulations! You now have your very own piece of sandstone.

Materials
- dry sand
- cementing solution (2 parts water to 1 part Epsom salts)
- paper cups
- paper towel

Did You Know?
Sandstone is classified as a sedimentary rock. Sedimentary rocks can take thousands of years to form. You made your very own in two days!

183 The Thirsty Brick

Investigate whether rocks can absorb water.

STEPS

1. Pour a measured amount of water into the container. Make sure you pour enough water so that it completely covers the brick.
2. Put the brick in the middle of the water-filled container. Can you see anything happening to the water level?
3. Leave the brick in the container for 45 minutes.
4. Remove the brick from the container. Make sure you allow the excess water to drain off before completely removing the brick.
5. Calculate how much water was soaked up by the brick. This can be done by pouring the excess water back into the measuring container. Subtract the remaining volume from the original volume. Your answer will be the amount of water absorbed by the brick.

Materials
- large plastic container
- measuring cup (must have level markings)
- brick

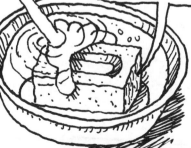

Did You Know?
Most rocks in the environment absorb water. However, the amount of water they can absorb depends on a number of factors. One factor is how absorbent the rock is.

184 Making Limestone

Make a piece of limestone.

STEPS

1. Line the shoe box with plastic.
2. Add the plaster and water, taking care to mix it thoroughly.
3. Add the shell pieces and thoroughly mix them in with the plaster.
4. Pour the mixture into the cups.
5. Place the cups in a warm area (i.e. a kitchen cabinet), where they will not be disturbed for three to four days.
6. Remove limestone from cups. Describe what the limestone looks and feels like.

Materials
- shoe box
- plastic garbage bag
- paper cups
- dry plaster
- water
- pieces of shells

Did You Know?
Limestone is a type of sedimentary rock made up mostly of calcium carbonate. When microscopic marine animals die, they fall to the sea floor where their hard parts (shells) collect and eventually form limestone.

---

185 Making Conglomerate Rock

Make a piece of conglomerate rock.

STEPS

1. Line the shoe box with plastic.
2. Add one cup of dry cement, one cup of dry sand, and one cup of cold water. Mix thoroughly.
3. Add rocks to the mixture and mix again.
4. Line the small cups with the sandwich bags and pour the mixture.
5. Place the cups in a warm area (i.e. a kitchen cabinet) until the mixture is dry. Describe the texture of the rock.

I've made my own piece of conglomerate rock. Just like a chip off the old block!

Materials
- shoe box
- plastic garbage bag
- paper cups
- sandwich bags
- dry cement
- dry sand
- water
- rocks

Did You Know?
Conglomerate rock is a rock made up of particles of different sizes. Rocks are made up of minerals. Scientists classify different types of rock according to their grain size and what each rock is made up of.

186 At-home Paleontologist

Make your very own fossilized footprint.

STEPS

1. Carefully cut a milk carton lengthwise.
2. Fill the cut milk carton with a layer of sand about 2¼ in (6 cm) deep.
3. Place one foot on top of the sand, and carefully press down so that your footprint remains on the sand.
4. Fill the small cup with plaster and pour it into the larger cup. Repeat. Add one small cup of water and let the mixture sit until all of the water has been absorbed. The plaster will be the pretend mud that is needed in the fossilization process.
5. After the plaster has been mixed, carefully pour it into the milk carton. Make sure to completely cover the footprint with plaster.
6. After the plaster has set, carefully lift your fossilized footprint out of the sand and give it a quick clean. Now you can compare your plaster fossil to the original footprint.

Materials
- a 4 pint (2 L) milk or juice carton
- bucket of sand
- small cup
- large cup
- water
- plaster
- scissors

Did You Know?
Fossilized evidence is one method scientists use to discover what types of plants and animals lived many thousands of years ago. Without fossils we may have never known what type of dinosaurs once roamed our planet. If you visit your local museum you might find some real fossilized footprints on display.

187 Missing Footprints

Search for and fossilize footprints.

STEPS

1. Go outside to your yard or to a nearby park or the beach, and look for a footprint impression within the dirt or sand.
2. Although to us it is only a footprint made a few hours or a couple of days ago, paleontologists spend years looking for similar things.
3. Fill the small cup with plaster and pour it into the larger cup. Repeat (this will be the pretend mud that is needed to fossilize the footprint). Add one small cup of water and let the mixture sit until all of the water has been absorbed.
4. After the plaster has been mixed, carefully pour it into and over your footprint. Make sure you completely cover the footprint with the plaster mixture.
5. After the plaster has set, carefully lift up your fossilized footprint. Now you can compare your plaster footprint to the original footprint you found.

Materials
- small cup
- large cup
- water
- plaster
- brush
- footprint

Did You Know?
Some fossils, such as bone, may consist of the actual remains of the organism. However, most fossils consist only of the impression left in the rock by the organism after the remains have decomposed or dissolved.

Yes! A great footprint for my experiment but I'm starting to wonder just what lives around here!

GEOLOGY & GEOGRAPHY

GEOLOGY: THE STUDY OF THE EARTH INCLUDING COMPOSITION, STRUCTURE AND ORIGIN OF ITS ROCKS AND THE GEOLIGICAL FEATURES OF A DISTRICT.

GEOGRAPHY: THE STUDY OF THE EARTH'S PHYSICAL FEATURES, RESOURCES AND CLIMATE AND THE PHYSICAL ASPECTS OF ITS POPULATION.

Date:	Experiment:	Notes:

188 Digging for Dinosaurs

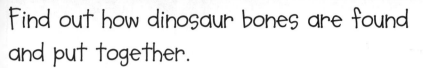

Find out how dinosaur bones are found and put together.

Materials
- dinosaur model
- 3–5 shoe boxes (or similar)
- friend

STEPS

1. Take your shoe boxes and cut some holes in the lids just big enough to put your hand through.
2. Invite your friend to place the pieces of the dinosaur model in the shoe boxes. Ask your friend to mix them up so that they are not in any order. (To be clever your friend could leave some out.)
3. Have your friend arrange the shoe boxes on the floor.
4. Now place your hand in the various boxes and pull out the pieces of dinosaur model. Can you put together a dinosaur from the pieces you have found?

Note: Your local museum might have a "skeleton" of a dinosaur created from fossilized bones and other materials (to fill in the gaps). Visit the museum and find out about these creatures that existed millions of years ago.

The head bone's connected to the neck bone …

WHY?

After an animal dies it eventually gets covered under layers of sand and earth. Over millions of years, water and minerals pass through the shell or bone and the chemicals in it change into a rock-like mixture of minerals. This is a fossil. Scientists can study fossils to find out what animals were alive during which period of time.

As a paleontologist I can tell this is a very old fossil of a … fish.

Did You Know?

The study of fossils and extinct animals and plants is called paleontology.

189 Soil Search

What lives in soil?

Materials
- small bucket of soil
- large bucket
- kitchen sieve
- magnifying glass
- pen and paper
- newspaper

STEPS

1. Go out to the yard and collect half a small bucket of soil.
2. Empty the contents of the small bucket, so the soil falls through the kitchen sieve and into the large bucket.
3. Spread out some newspaper and empty the contents of the sieve.
4. Using the pen and paper write down all the living things that you find in the soil.
5. Now write down all the non-living things that you find.

Note: Always wash your hands after handling dirt—or wear gloves. Why do you think this would be a good idea? (Think about what you found in the soil samples.)

Did You Know?

Although its chief component is weathered rock, dirt also contains water, air, bacteria, and decayed plant and animal materials. Did you find any of these?

190 What's in Dirt?

Examine different dirt samples.

Materials
- 3 medium-sized cups
- 3 kitchen sieves
- paper and pen

STEPS

1. Collect three different dirt samples.
2. Each dirt sample should be collected in a large cup.
3. The dirt samples should be taken from three different locations. Areas may include: a sandpile, near a pond or stream, or from a yard.
4. Each dirt sample should then be put through a kitchen sieve.
5. Make sure you hold onto what is left in the sieve. The dirt that passes through the sieve can then be put back.
6. Record what was found in each sieve. Were there many differences between the contents of the three sieves?

Note: Remember to wash your hands after handling dirt.

Did You Know?

Dirt is really made from the erosion of rocks. This process can take thousands of years. Just think, the dirt you collected today was once a big rock!

191 Rock Search

Find and group rocks according to texture, grain size, and color.

STEPS

1. Place the drop sheet over your workspace. Spread out your rocks and look them over.
2. Group your rocks according to color. One group should contain light-colored rocks, the other group should contain dark-colored rocks.
3. Group your rocks according to texture. One group should contain rocks that have a fine or smooth texture. The other group should contain rocks with a coarse or rough texture.
4. Now using your magnifying glass, group your rocks according to their grain size. One group should contain the rocks with the small or fine grains. The other group should contain the rocks with the larger grains.

Materials
- rock collection (6–10 rocks should be sufficient)
- paper
- pen
- drop sheet
- magnifying glass

Did You Know?
The rocks that make up the world's continents are all made of minerals. About 5,000 different minerals have been identified in Earth's crust.

192 Rock Hunt

Identify and group rocks.

STEPS

1. Go outside or to a nearby park or beach.
2. Collect six rocks, making sure they are all collected from different areas (a garden, next to a lake, or from the school sports field).
3. Write down all the differences that you can spot between all of the rocks.
4. Do you think that the different locations where the rocks were found account for any of the differences identified?

Materials
- rock collection
- pen
- paper

Did You Know?
Meteorites, which are rocks from space, help scientists learn about the solar system and are very valuable too!

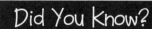

193 At-home Volcano

Make your very own working volcano.

STEPS

1. Sculpt the modeling clay so that it forms the shape of a volcano.
2. Make a hole in the top of the volcano. The hole should be big enough so that the empty film canister can fit into it.
3. Insert the empty film canister into the hole.
4. Now it is time to add the ingredients that form the flowing "molten lava." You might need to ask an adult for help.
5. First add a tablespoon of baking soda to the empty canister. Now add the vinegar. Step back and watch your volcano come to life.

Materials
- modeling clay
- empty film canister
- tablespoon of baking soda
- tablespoon of vinegar

Did You Know?

Volcanoes erupt every day someplace on Earth. The Stromboli volcano near southern Italy is erupting this very minute, as are less famous, continually active volcanoes in Ethiopia, Indonesia, and elsewhere. The next big eruption will be ... we don't know where!

---

194 Volcano in the Sandpile!

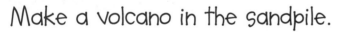

Make a volcano in the sandpile.

STEPS

1. Sculpt a volcano out of sand in the sandpile.
2. Dig a hole in the top of the volcano. The hole should be big enough so that an empty film canister can fit into it.
3. Insert the empty film canister into the hole.
4. Now it is time to make the volcano explode.
5. First add a tablespoon of baking soda into the empty canister and the food dye. Now add the vinegar.
6. Step back and watch your volcano come to life.

Materials
- sandpile
- empty film canister
- baking soda
- vinegar
- food dye

Did You Know?

The biggest volcano on Earth is Mauna Loa on the island of Hawaii, in the middle of the Pacific Ocean. The largest underwater volcano is Tamu Massif, 1,000 miles (1,600 km) east of Japan and it's 60× bigger than Mauna Loa.

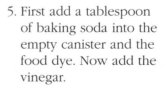

Everybody out of the sandpile!

195 That's Volcanic!

Show how pressure can cause a volcanic eruption.

Materials
- metal funnel
- modeling clay (you will only need a small amount)
- frying pan
- water

STEPS

1. Take the metal funnel and cover the narrow end with a very thin strip of modeling clay. (You might need help with this.)
2. Take your frying pan, fill it a third full with water, and place it on the stove.
3. Heat the water.
4. Place the funnel wide-end down in the water.
5. Turn up the heat and stand clear!

Did You Know?
One of the earliest detailed reports of a volcanic eruption was by Pliny the Younger. He wrote about the eruption of Mount Vesuvius in AD 79, which was the cause of the destruction of Pompeii. Pompeii is still being excavated today for information about how the Romans lived.

196 Lava Icing

See how lava flows and creates different types of rocks at different temperatures.

Materials
- 1 lb (450 g) of icing
- 2 bowls
- 2 plates

STEPS

1. Make your icing.
2. Divide the icing evenly between the two bowls.
3. Leave one of the bowls on the bench and put the other in the refrigerator.
4. Take the bowl from the refrigerator when the icing has cooled but is still able to be poured.
5. On one of the plates pour the warm mixture, on the other pour the cool mixture. What do you notice about how the icing pours?

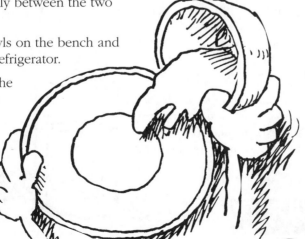

Did You Know?
Magma (molten rock) can reach a temperature of about 2,372°F (1,300°C). Not only that, volcanoes can produce different kinds of rocks including basalt, granite, and obsidian.

197 Float or Sink?

Can you predict which rock will float or sink?

STEPS

1. Take your pen and paper and predict which rocks will float and which rocks will sink. Write your prediction down.
2. Fill the plastic container with water.
3. Drop all your rocks into the container.
4. How many did you get right? How many did your friends get?

Did You Know?
Diamond is the hardest rock and granite is the second hardest.

Materials
- pumice stone (the bathroom might have one)
- small piece of sandstone
- small piece of granite
- small brick or small piece of cement
- clear plastic container
- enough water to just fill the plastic container
- pen
- paper

---

198 Which Rock is the Thirstiest?

Identify what type of rock is most porous.

STEPS

1. Measure and pour the same amount of water into the three containers.
2. Make note of how much water was poured into each container.
3. Put one rock in the middle of each water-filled container.
4. Make sure there is enough water to cover each rock completely.
5. Ensure you leave each rock in the water for at least 30 minutes. Can you see anything happening to the water level?
6. Carefully remove the rocks from their containers. Make sure you allow all of the excess water to drain into the container.
7. Calculate how much water was soaked up by each rock. This can be done by pouring the excess water back into the measuring container and subtracting this volume from the original volume.

Materials
- 3 large, clear-plastic containers
- measuring cup
- piece of granite
- piece of sandstone
- piece of limestone

Did You Know?
The color of granite ranges from pink to light gray.

199 The Amazing Floating Rock

Can a rock float on water?

"In goes my piece of Mt. Vesuvius. Now let's see what happens."

STEPS

1. Fill the clear-plastic container with water.
2. Drop the pumice stone into the container.
3. Does it sink to the bottom or float to the top?

Materials
- pumice stone (the bathroom might have one)
- clear-plastic container
- enough water to just fill the plastic container

Did You Know?

The pumice stone can be used to get rid of all those yucky bits found on your feet. It is actually made from rock which is found only in volcanoes!

---

200 Volcanic "Mud"

Lava is molten rock. See what it does when it is very hot.

STEPS

1. Mix your gravy mix with some water in a bowl. (Follow the recipe on the packet.)
2. Place the pan on the stove and tip the mixture into it. (Ask an adult to help you.)
3. Heat it up. Watch what happens. Do you see bubbles rising to the surface?

"Volcanic mud for dinner? What else would rocks eat?"

Materials
- gravy mix
- water
- pan

Did You Know?

This is the way volcanic mud reacts when it is hot. The mud is so hot that it forces the air in it to the top. This is a very volatile substance. When lava cools it forms rocks full of little holes.

201 The Slow-moving Glacier

Demonstrate the movement of a glacier using a block of ice as a model.

STEPS

1. The first step is to make miniature glaciers.
2. Fill the zip-lock bags with water. Do not fill them right to the top, otherwise they will burst while freezing.
3. Before zip locking the bag add some twigs and pebbles.
4. Zip lock the bag, and put it into the freezer. Leave it there overnight or until the water is frozen.
5. Once it is frozen, remove the bag by simply ripping the plastic off. You have just made your very own, miniature glacier.
6. Go outside and find an asphalt or concrete area that has a slight decline.
7. Push down on the ice block and watch it move slowly forward as it melts.
8. Make note of the debris left behind. Real glaciers change Earth's crust in much the same way, but on a much bigger scale.

Materials
- medium-sized zip-lock bags
- handful of pebbles
- handful of twigs
- water
- freezer

Did You Know?
Every continent on Earth has glaciers, except Australia. Australia did have glaciers thousands of years ago, but with the onset of global warming they all melted away in much the same way as your miniature glacier!

202 Rubbing the Glacial Way

See how glaciers affect the surface of Earth.

STEPS

1. Spread some newspaper so that your work area stays clean.
2. Place the modeling clay on the ground and flatten it out.
3. Take an ice cube and rub it over the surface of the clay. What do you notice happening?
4. Sprinkle some sand on the clay and rub an ice cube over it. Is the effect the same or different to when you rubbed the ice on the clay without the sand?

Materials
- 1–2 ice cubes
- cup of sand
- modeling clay
- newspaper

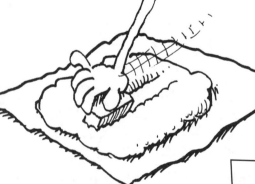

Did You Know?
Almost ten percent of Earth is covered by glaciers. During the last Ice Age 32 percent of Earth was covered by glaciers—that's a lot of ice!

203 Metamorphic Pancakes

Find out how metamorphic rock is formed.

Materials
- pancake mix
- raisins
- coconut
- nuts
- frying pan
- stove

STEPS

1. Make up your pancake mix following the recipe. (You might need help to do this.)
2. Now add in some raisins, some coconut, and some nuts. What you have made is similar to sedimentary rock.
3. Now heat your pan and fry your pancake. What has happened? Has the pancake hardened and taken a specific shape?

Who'd like their pancake like metamorphic rock? Well, that's what I'm making!

Did You Know?

Metamorphic rock is sedimentary rock changed by heat caused by the pressure of the upper layers of the Earth. Look at rocks in cliffs or along the shore at the beach. If you can see different layers, this is sedimentary rock. It takes thousands of years to form. Your pancake took just a few minutes!

204 Home-made Geodes

Find out about the rocks called geodes by making some.

Materials
- Epsom salts
- 2 cups of warm water
- eggshell halves
- food dye (different colors if you like)

STEPS

1. Spoon Epsom salts into the warm water until no more will dissolve. (Ask an adult to help.)
2. Add food dye to the solution.
3. Pour this solution into the eggshell halves and leave the water to evaporate. (This may take a few days, so be patient.)
4. When the water has evaporated you have made your very own geodes!

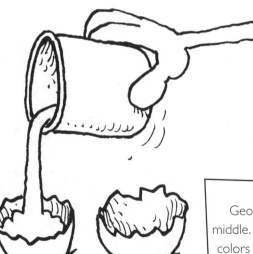

Did You Know?

Geodes are sphere-like stones with crystals in the middle. Sometimes the crystals inside can be of different colors because of the different minerals that are inside the rock. If you can, find a whole real geode and break it open. You will be surprised at what you find inside. Sometimes these stones are displayed at museums. Look for these when you visit your local museum.

205 Magnetic Rocks

Sometimes the minerals in rocks can make them magnetic.

Materials
- sheet of cardboard
- rocks
- magnet

STEPS

1. Collect some rocks from your yard. Find as many different types of rock as you can.
2. Place the rocks on your cardboard. Spread them out.
3. Now place your magnet close to each of the rocks. Are some attracted to the magnet and others not?

Did You Know?

There are many different types of minerals in rocks. The rocks that are attracted to your magnet have iron in them. This is why they move to the magnet.

206 This is Very Hard!

Test the hardness of different minerals.

Materials
- piece of quartz
- piece of soapstone
- coin
- nail
- your fingernail

STEPS

1. Take your mineral specimens and lay them on a table.
2. With your fingernail try to scratch the surface of each of the rocks. (Be careful not to hurt yourself.)
3. With the coin try to scratch the surface of each of the rocks. Which ones were difficult to scratch?
4. Finally, try to scratch the surface of each of the rocks with the nail. (Be very careful this time.)
5. Now place the rocks in a line from softest to hardest.

Scratch this piece of quartz with my fingernail? I don't have any fingernails. I'm just a character in a book!

Did You Know?

Rocks are different from minerals. Minerals are made up of one substance only, whereas rocks are made up of many minerals. The largest rock in the world is Uluru in the Northern Territory, Australia.

207 Dishing up the Crystals

See how crystals are formed.

STEPS

1. Warm two or three cups of water in the pan.
2. Stir the Epsom salts into the water until no more will dissolve.
3. Tip the water into the bowl and add the two pieces of charcoal.
4. Now leave your bowl in a safe place and check it over the next five days. Have crystals formed in your dish?
5. This experiment could be repeated using alum or copper sulfate (which is poisonous, so wash your hands). You will see differently shaped crystals form.

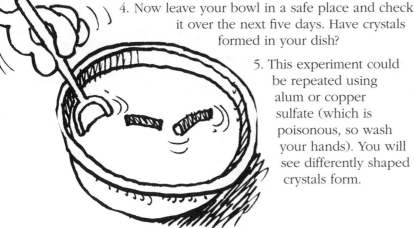

Materials
- pan
- 1 lb (450g) of Epsom salts
- bowl
- 2 pieces of charcoal
- spoon
- warm water

Did You Know?
Gems get their color from the minerals from which they are formed. Out of all the minerals in the world there are only a few that produce the beautiful colors of gems.

---

208 Crystal on a String

You can grow a crystal on a string.

STEPS

1. Warm the water in the pan on a low heat. (You might need help with this.)
2. Add salt, alum, or sugar to the water until no more will dissolve.
3. Leave this to cool so the crystals will form.
4. Take out the largest crystal and add as much salt to the solution as the crystal displaced.
5. Heat the solution again until the salt dissolves.
6. Cool this solution and pour it into a narrow glass.
7. Tie the thread around the crystal and place it in the solution. Leave. What do you notice after a number of days?

Materials
- salt (you can also use alum or sugar)
- pan
- narrow glass
- string about 12 in (30 cm) long
- water
- stove

Did You Know?
The study of caves is called speleology.

209 Stalagmite or Stalactite?

How are stalagmites and stalactites formed?

STEPS

1. Warm the water in the pan and add in salt until no more will dissolve.
2. Place the glasses about 6 in (15 cm) apart and put the plate in between.
3. Now place one end of the string in one glass of water and the other end in the other one.
4. Pour the salty solution into the glasses in even amounts and leave it for at least three days. If the experiment has worked there should be crystals hanging from the string and underneath it.

Note: Stala<u>c</u>tites hang from the <u>c</u>eiling. Stala<u>g</u>mites grow up from the <u>g</u>round.

Did You Know?

A stalagmite is a pointed rock formation formed by rock dripping down from above. The force of gravity pulling molten rock downward causes a stalactite.

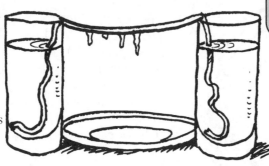

Materials
- Epsom salts (you can also use alum or sugar)
- pan
- 2 glasses
- string about 16 in (40 cm) long
- water
- small plate

210 Fizzin' Minerals

Investigate how various minerals react to vinegar.

STEPS

1. Fill your bowl with vinegar.
2. Place the granite in the vinegar. What happens? Remove the granite.
3. Next, place the sandstone in the vinegar. What happens? Remove the sandstone.
4. Finally, place the limestone in the vinegar. What happens? Does it fizz?

Materials
- piece each of granite, sandstone, and limestone
- vinegar
- bowl

Did You Know?

Some minerals react to acids, such as vinegar, whereas other minerals don't react at all. The limestone in your experiment actually gives off a gas when it comes into contact with vinegar.

211 Minerals, Minerals Everywhere

Discover how minerals are part of our lives.

STEPS

1. Take your pen and paper.
2. Now wander around your home and write down anything that you think is made from minerals.
3. Make a list as long as you can and check it with an adult.

Hints: Do you have salt in your kitchen? What is your stove made of? What is in your pencil?

Materials
- pen
- paper
- your eyesight

Did You Know?
Diamonds are the hardest things known to scientists. They are also used to make laser beams as they affect light in a certain way.

212 Making Pet Rocks

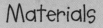

Have some creative fun with different kinds of rocks.

STEPS

1. Spread the newspaper on the ground.
2. Put the rocks out on the newspaper.
3. Look at the rocks. Do you notice any differences between the rocks?
4. Take your paint and materials and go for it!
5. You might even create a "rock concert."

Materials
- rocks
- paint
- markers
- things to decorate a rock with, i.e. string for hair, buttons for eyes etc.
- newspaper
- glue

Did You Know?
There are three different types of rocks—sedimentary, metamorphic, and igneous.

213 What's in Sand

What can you find in sand?

STEPS

1. Put your sand samples in different bowls.
2. Add vinegar to each bowl so that the sand is covered.
3. What happens to your sand samples after you add the vinegar?
4. If you noticed a reaction in one, it is because the vinegar has affected some shells in one of your samples.

Materials
- different types of sand (coarse and fine sand)
- vinegar
- bowls (1 bowl for each type of sand)

Did You Know?
Sand is made up of rocks that have been worn down, but it can also contain shells washed up from the sea. Shells are the remains of dead sea animals.

---

214 Chalk Talk

How do acids affect minerals?

STEPS

1. Take the piece of chalk and place it in the glass with a little vinegar.
2. Leave for five to ten minutes.
3. Now check the chalk. What has happened to it?

Materials
- chalk
- drinking glass
- vinegar

Did You Know?
Chalk is made from a type of mineral called calcium carbonate. This mineral dissolves when it comes into contact with an acid like vinegar. Chemical reactions, like the one you have performed, can also happen on Earth to produce geographical structures.

215 Hey, You're Blocking My Funnel!

See how clay absorbs water.

STEPS

1. Put the funnel in the glass.
2. Now put some clay into the funnel. (Make sure all the edges are covered.)
3. Tip some water into the funnel. What happens?
4. Leave the clay for a while and check it again in half an hour. Can you see any water coming through?

Materials
- clay from the back yard (you might need help to find a sample)
- funnel
- drinking glass
- water

Did You Know?

Clay has very small particles that are very tightly held together. Ground that becomes waterlogged may have a lot of clay in it. Clay is a very common material found in soil.

---

216 Pretend Panning

See how panning for gold works.

STEPS

1. Fill the tray with water to a shallow level.
2. Pour the birdseed into the water.
3. Take your colander and scoop some of the birdseed out of the water.
4. Shake your colander so that the small particles fall through the holes while the larger ones remain. Pick out a particular type of seed. This is your pretend gold.
5. Repeat this process until you have a pile of seed.
6. When you have finished take the pile of seed and paint it gold. When the paint has dried, pan for your "real" gold this time.

Wow! Look! Real gold birdseed!

Materials
- birdseed
- sieve or colander
- flat tray
- water
- gold paint

Did You Know?

Gold fossickers pan for gold in this way because gold can be found in riverbeds. The gold travels through the water and ends up in the stones and rocks of the river. Good sized pieces of gold can be found using the process of panning. Gold is also heavier than pieces of rock or sand. Particles of gold will sink to the bottom and will be found when the rocky pieces and sand have been swished away with water.

217 Rock or Not!

Identify buildings made from rocks.

STEPS

1. With an adult and some friends, walk around your local area and try to identify which of the buildings are made from rock.
2. Write down which buildings you think are made from rock and which are not. Mark where they are on your map.
3. Get together with your friends and discuss your answers.
4. Remember, buildings made from sandstone, bluestone, and granite are made from rock. Buildings made with brick and cement are not made from rock.

An unusual building for our local area—but it is definitely made from stone.

Materials
- pen
- paper
- map of your local area

Did You Know?

The rocks that make up the world's continents are all made of minerals. Manufactured materials such as brick, plastic, plaster, and cement are not minerals because they are not natural in origin. Therefore, they are not considered rocks.

218 Journey to the Middle of the Earth

Simulate the sections of Earth's interior using an apple.

STEPS

1. Cut the apple in half from the stem, through the core, to the base.
2. Press one half of the apple onto the ink pad and carefully place it onto the large piece of paper.
3. Leave the apple on the paper for a few seconds while applying a little pressure.
4. Carefully remove the apple from the paper. You should now have an ink imprint of the apple.
5. Do you notice any similarities between your stamp of the apple and that of Earth's interior?
6. Finish off by tagging your stamp. Write in where you think Earth's crust would be on your stamp. Also, fill in where you think Earth's core and mantle would be.

Materials
- apple
- knife
- ink pad
- large sheet of paper
- pen
- ruler

Did You Know?

The Earth's outermost surface is called the crust. The crust is typically about 25 miles (40 km) thick beneath the continents, and about 6 miles (10 km) thick beneath the oceans. On your ink model the crust was represented by just the apple skin!

219 Melting Polar Ice Caps

If the polar ice caps melted, would the sea level rise?

STEPS

1. The ice in this experiment represents the polar ice caps. Empty the tray of ice cubes into the cup. Filling the cup halfway should be sufficient for this experiment to work.

2. Carefully fill the cup with water. Try to get the water level as close to the rim of the cup as possible without overfilling it. The water in this experiment represents the oceans of the world.

3. Now, wait for the polar ice caps (the ice) to melt. Predict what you think will happen. Do you think the water will rise and overflow, stay the same, or decrease?

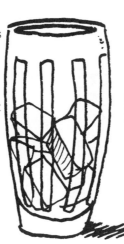

Materials
- tray of ice blocks
- large cup (milkshake cup is perfect)
- enough water to fill the cup

Did You Know?
It is not the melting polar ice caps that will contribute to the rising of the sea level. The major contributor will be the snow melting from the mountain areas, such as the Himalayas.

220 Biodegradable Bags

Compare the biodegradability of a plastic bag and a paper bag.

STEPS

1. With permission, use the shovel to dig two small holes in your yard. Make sure that the holes are no farther than 3 ft (1 m) apart and approximately 8 in (20 cm) deep (you might need help to do this).

2. Place the plastic bag in one hole and the paper bag in the other hole.

3. Fill both holes with soil, ensuring that they are fully covered. Place a marker such as an ice cream stick to show where the bags are buried.

4. Now all you have to do is leave the bags covered for a month.

5. Come back after a month and dig up both bags. Which bag has biodegraded the most?

Materials
- plastic shopping bag
- paper bag (preferably the same size as the plastic bag)
- shovel
- yard
- 2 ice cream sticks

Did You Know?
The biggest problem with plastic bags is that they do not readily break down. It has been estimated that it takes between 20 to 1,000 years for them to decompose. I wonder how long your bag will take?

221 Making Mountains Last

Find out how structures made of different materials are affected by water.

Materials
- dirt
- sand
- rocks
- drinking glass or cup
- water

STEPS

1. In your back yard, build three mountains: one from rocks; one from sand; and one from dirt. Make the mountains as secure as you can.
2. Fill the glass with water. Pour the water over the mountain made from rocks. What happens?
3. Repeat step 2 but this time pour the water over the mountain made of dirt. What happens?
4. Finally, pour some water over the mountain made of sand. What happens this time?

Did You Know?
Different materials in the Earth are affected in different ways by rain and water. This is one way that different land formations come about.

222 Hey, I'm Eroding Away!

See how water causes erosion.

Materials
- two clear flat patches of earth
- drinking glass
- water

STEPS

1. Clear a section of ground in your backyard. Flatten out the ground so that it is even.
2. Fill your glass with water. Hold it at a height of about 6 in (15 cm) from the ground and pour the water. Note what happens.
3. Now fill your glass with water again. On another spot of cleared earth pour the water, this time from a height of about 12 in (30 cm) from the earth. Is the result the same? Did the water affect the earth differently?

Did You Know?
The effect of water on land is to erode it away. When land is cleared of trees and bush, the soil is eroded much more quickly because the trees and bush hold the earth together. Soil erosion is a big environmental problem.

223 Eggs Continental

Find out how Earth's tectonic plates work.

Materials
- boiled egg

STEPS

1. Take the boiled egg and crack it on its side. (What you want are two or three large pieces of eggshell, not a lot of little shards.) Note the way the outside of the egg looks.

2. Take your egg and try to move the pieces of the shell horizontally around the egg so that the pieces move against each other.

3. Do the pieces of shell move over each other? Do they buckle or move upward?

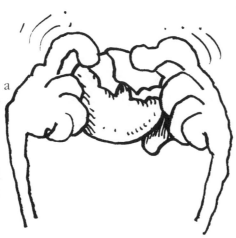

Did You Know?

You have made something similar to the surface of Earth in this experiment, with your shell being what is called tectonic plates. Earth's surface is actually made up of these plates, which move at the rate of about 2 in (4 cm) a year. This movement is called continental drift. A sudden shift between these tectonic plates can result in an earthquake.

---

224 My Crust is Bent!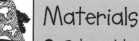

See how earthquakes affect Earth's surface.

Materials
- 2 long blocks of wood
- modeling clay
- rolling pin
- marker

STEPS

1. Place the two blocks together.
2. Roll out the clay so it will cover both the blocks of wood.
3. Cover the blocks with the clay.
4. If you like, you can draw a road on the clay.
5. Move one of the blocks in one direction against the other block. What happens to the clay?

Did You Know?

Earthquakes happen when two plates in the Earth's crust, moving against each other, slip. This is why they occur frequently in places where two tectonic plates meet.

225 A Sedimentary Situation

Make and examine sedimentary rock.

STEPS

1. Half fill the jar with water.
2. Pour in a layer of cement about 1½ in (4 cm) deep.
3. Leave for a few days.
4. Pour in another layer, this time of sand mixed with cement. Allow to harden.
5. Pour in another layer, this time of plaster and sand. Allow to harden.
6. Pour in some water and food dye.
7. Pour in another layer of plaster and sand. Allow to harden.
8. Remove the glass. (Ask an adult to do this.) You have made your own sedimentary rock.

Materials
- large glass jar
- cement
- sand
- plaster
- water
- food dye

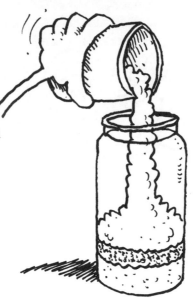

Did You Know?
Sedimentary rock makes up the upper layers of the Earth. It is not as hard as rock found deeper in the Earth and has a high content of sand.

226 Watch Out for the Quicksand

Investigate how quicksand works and discover its interesting qualities.

STEPS

1. Fill the bowl about halfway with cornstarch.
2. Add water to it and stir thoroughly until it makes a thick paste. This is your "quicksand."
3. Now with two fingers pretend to "walk" across the quicksand. Do it quickly first. Did you make it across the quicksand?
4. Now try to walk across the quicksand slowly. Can you make it across this time?
5. Put a stone on your "quicksand." See how quickly it sinks.

Materials
- cornstarch
- water
- bowl

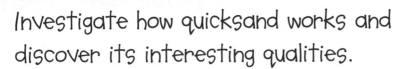

Did You Know?
Quicksand is a mixture of water and sand. In real life, quicksand can be dangerous because the surface of it looks hard and solid but when it is walked on objects sink into it.

227 Mapping the Ocean Floor

How can you map a surface?

Did You Know?
The technical term for the instrument used to measure a landscape in this way is a probe. The ocean floor was once mapped in this way, using long lines with lead weights on the bottom. Today oceanographers use radars or sonar.

Materials
- large lunch box
- chopstick
- ruler
- modeling clay
- 2 pieces of cardboard (large enough to cover the lunch box)
- friend

STEPS

1. Ask your friend to construct a landscape, with mountains and a valley, inside the lunch box using the modeling clay.

2. Now ask your friend to cover the lunch box with the two pieces of cardboard so that there is a small gap lengthways down the lunch box. This gap should be big enough to put the chopstick through, but not so wide that you can see into the lunch box.

3. Put your chopstick into the box at different points along the length of the box. Each time you do this (you probably only need to do it three or four times) measure with the ruler how much of the chopstick can be seen above the cardboard. Make sure that your chopstick is always straight up.

4. From your measurements, can you get an idea of some of the physical aspects of the bottom of the lunch box? Did you find high places? Did you find low places?

---

228 Wondrous Woodchips

See how convection makes currents in the oceans.

Did You Know?
This process is called convection. The ocean currents are created by convection because some water is very cold near the North and South Poles, and some water is very warm near the equator. This causes the water to move around the Earth's surface.

Materials
- plastic lunch box
- heat source (perhaps a stove)
- tray of ice
- woodchips
- 2 different shades of food dye

STEPS

1. Put the end of the lunch box near the heat source and put the ice at the other end. Half fill the lunch box with water.

2. Put one of the food dyes at one end of the lunch box and the other at the other end of the lunch box. What happens?

3. Now drop the woodchips gently into the lunch box. What happens to them?

229 Avalanche!

Find out how different materials can be stable, or unstable and cause an avalanche.

Did You Know?
Avalanches are caused by a weakening of the bond between layers of earth or snow. This weakening causes the earth or snow on the top to slide down, making an avalanche. Avalanches can occur very suddenly and unexpectedly.

Materials
- 2 lb (1 kg) sugar
- 2 lb (1 kg) flour
- 10 oz (280 g) dried coconut
- piece of cardboard 24 in × 24 in (60 cm × 60 cm)
- newspaper

STEPS

1. Go outside and spread the newspaper on the ground so it covers a space wider than the size of the cardboard.
2. Take your piece of cardboard and lay it flat on the newspaper.
3. In layers, place some sugar, coconut, and flour in any order on the cardboard. Make a note of the order in which you layered them.
4. Raise the cardboard and note how your materials fall.
5. Repeat these steps two or three times but layer your materials in a different order each time. (Remember to note the order in which you layered them.)
6. Which combination made the best "avalanche'?
7. Record your results.

230 Slidin' Mudslides

See how earth can slide down a mountain.

Materials
- newspaper
- piece of canvas
- half a bucket of sand and gravel
- water
- bucket
- 4 bricks

STEPS

1. Scrunch up the newspaper so that you have enough to make a steady pile about 8 in (20 cm) high.
2. On some flat ground outside, pile up your newspaper to make the shape of a mountain.
3. Cover the newspaper with some canvas and secure it with bricks. This is your mountain so make it a little uneven like a real mountain.
4. In the bucket, mix the soil and gravel with water to make mud.
5. Now pour the mud over your mountain. How does the mud flow down the mountain? Did it flow in the way you expected?

Did You Know?
Mudslides can often be caused by deforestation. This is when a mountain has had all of its trees removed. When the environment is changed in this way it can have disastrous results, for example, a mudslide.

231 Making Rivers

See how rivers and lakes are formed.

STEPS

1. Crumple up the paper, but not too tightly.
2. Stretch it out now and tape it about 1 in (2.5 cm) within the border of the cardboard. It should make a mountainous-looking region.
3. Put some water in your spray bottle and add the food dye.
4. Now spray water over the paper. Can you see rivers forming on the paper? Try spraying a little harder. What happens now?

Materials
- sheet of paper
- sheet of same-sized cardboard
- spray bottle
- water
- food dye

Did You Know?
Some famous rivers are the Amazon, the Nile, and the Yangtze. These rivers took thousands of years to form. Can you find these rivers in your atlas?

232 Play-doh Mountains

See how the Earth is affected by different forces that can create mountains.

STEPS

1. Take your modeling clay and on the newspaper roll it into a long shape like a cylinder.
2. From both ends, push the clay together. Does it rise in the middle?
3. Roll your clay out again but this time pull it apart from the ends. What happens now?
4. Finally, shape your clay into a rectangle. Hold one edge of the rectangle in each hand and push them toward each other. What shape is made in the clay now?

Materials
- large amount of soft modeling clay
- newspaper

Did You Know?
You have simulated what happens to the Earth because of the movement of the tectonic plates. These plates move very slowly and force the Earth in different directions to form mountains and valleys.

233 A Home-made Seismograph

Make a device for measuring earth tremors.

STEPS

1. Stand the shoe box up on its end and place the can on the bottom in the box so it sits firmly.
2. Tape the lid of the shoe box to the end raised in the air so that it makes an upside-down L shape.
3. Tape the weights to the pointed end of your pencil. Make sure they are secure.
4. Tie one end of the string securely to the other end of the pencil.
5. On the shoe box lid, at the end sticking out, make a small hole and thread the other end of the string through.
6. Tie this end of string to the middle of the pen and sit the pen flat on top of the shoe box lid. You must make sure that the pencil hangs down so that its tip is level with the bottom of the shoe box.
7. Place your seismograph on a table and place a piece of paper under the pencil.
8. Shake the table gently. Are you getting a reading on your home-made seismograph?

Materials
- shoe box with lid
- pencil
- pen
- weights
- tape
- can of fruit or vegetables
- string

Did You Know?
This is the way that earthquakes are measured. There is also a scale to make a distinction between earthquakes of different intensity. This scale is called the Richter scale.

234 Settle Down, Pencil!

See how seismographs work.

STEPS

1. Take your materials when you go for your next trip in the car.
2. Get seated (don't forget to put your seat belt on) and place the firm flat object on your lap with the paper on top.
3. Hold the pencil in your hand so it is just touching the paper. Don't hold it too firmly but so that it can react readily to the movement of the car.
4. Do this as the car moves. What kind of picture have you made?

Would you mind taking the bumpiest, roughest road you can find please? The bumpier the better!

I'd like to see my seismograph go right off the scale!

Materials
- pencil
- sheet of paper
- something firm to rest your paper on
- trip in the car

Did You Know?
Seismographs work in a similar way to your experiment but they react to the movement of the Earth and measure earthquakes.

235 Mapping It Out

Understand how maps are made and make one of your own.

Materials
- ruler
- bedroom
- pencil
- sheet of paper
- large piece of paper
- piece of note paper

STEPS

1. The first thing you need to do is make a legend. A legend is an explanation of the symbols placed on a map. On your sheet of paper draw a picture of all the things in your room. Next to each object draw a symbol, i.e. next to the picture of a desk draw a square, next to the chairs draw an "x", and so on.

2. Now you need to measure the distances between various objects in the room. Use your ruler for this and take note of your measurements.

3. Now you need to draw the objects in the room onto your sheet of paper. Use your legend to represent the objects in the room. Because the sheet of paper is smaller than the room you need to "scale" the distances down. To scale your measurements down divide them by ten. If the measurements are still too large, divide them by a larger number.

4. Draw the objects in the room onto your map.

5. How accurate is your map? Could you navigate around the room using the map?

Did You Know?
All maps have a legend and a scale so that they can be read accurately. Have you ever seen a map of your city? Look at your street directory. Find your address.

236 Wall of Water

See if you can make your own wall of water.

Materials
- deep baking pan
- water
- blocks of wood

STEPS

1. Fill the pan with water and take it outside to a grassy area.

2. Place the two blocks of wood in the pan (they must be completely covered by the water).

3. Hold the blocks and move them together quickly.

4. Do this again and again until the blocks can no longer squeeze the water.

5. Watch how the movement of the blocks coming together quickly under the water forces swells of water to the surface. These make waves that splash over the sides of the pan.

Did You Know?
The action of the blocks and the water is like the conditions in the ocean that make a tsunami. Tsunami is the Japanese word for "harbor wave." It is a series of waves made by an earthquake below the ocean floor. The waves sometimes have enough energy to travel across a whole ocean! Tsunamis get higher as they reach shallow water. They can be very destructive. Type "tsunami" into Google on your computer and read about them.

237 Smog Alert

Smog is a pollution problem. See how it is made.

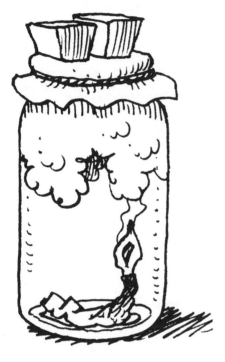

STEPS

1. Cut a strip of paper about 10 in (25 cm) by ½ in (1 cm).
2. Fold the strip in half along its length and twist the paper.
3. Make a lid that will seal the glass jar using the foil and put it aside for the moment.
4. Put some water in the jar. Swirl it around so the inside of the jar is wet, then pour out the water.
5. Place 3 ice cubes on top of the foil lid to make it cold.
6. Ask for help to set alight the strip of paper. Drop it and the match into the jar.
7. Replace the foil lid quickly and seal it tightly. Keep the ice cubes on top of the foil.
8. Record what you see in the jar. You will have made smog.

Materials
- glass jar
- water
- kitchen foil
- ice cubes
- paper
- scissors
- matches

I seem to be caught up in a smog experiment of some kind.

AAHURRGH

WHY?

Smog is a reaction between sunlight and industrial emissions, such as the burning of coal. Photochemical smog is a mixture of highly reactive chemicals that leave airborne particles which are dangerous to people and the environment. Smog mainly affects cities but can be carried in the wind to other areas.

Did You Know?

Smog is a mixture of natural fog (tiny droplets of water in the air), carbon dioxide, and smoke from pollution. It forms a thick, dirty, smelly atmosphere. Smog is harmful to people, animals, and plants.

238 Jar Compass

The Earth is a magnet. See how it works.

Materials
- needle
- magnet
- scissors
- small piece of cardboard
- jar
- thread
- pencil
- compass

STEPS

1. Stroke the needle with the magnet to magnetize it.
2. Tie one end of the string to the small piece of cardboard and the other end to the pencil.
3. Push the needle through the piece of cardboard.
4. Suspend the piece of cardboard inside the jar by lying the pencil across the mouth of the jar so the string is dangling. Do not allow the cardboard to touch the bottom.
5. The needle should lie horizontally. You should try to get the middle of the needle to rest in the middle of the cardboard.
6. Leave to stand freely and the needle should point in the same direction as the compass.

Did You Know?

The magnetized needle is free to turn on its own and will always point north and south. The needle is acting as a magnet and is attracted to Earth's magnetic force.

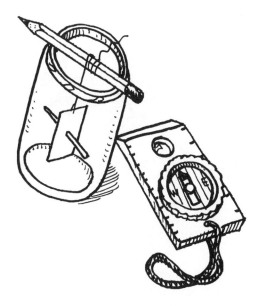

WHY?

The two ends of a magnet are called poles. Magnets can be used as powerful tools because two north-seeking, or two south-seeking, poles of a magnet will always repel each other, and a north-seeking and a south-seeking pole will always attract each other. Magnets are used in electrical motors and generators that power everyday items such as televisions, computers, and telephones.

239 A Homemade Stethoscope

See how sound waves can travel through enclosed spaces.

STEPS

1. Place one of the funnels into one end of the garden hose. If it doesn't fit tightly, secure it with some modeling clay.
2. Repeat this process with the other end of the hose.
3. Place one end of the funnel over your heart, and the other over your ear. What can you hear?

Materials
- 2 funnels
- length of garden hose about 16 in (40 cm) in length
- modeling clay

Did You Know?
A stethoscope can measure the rate of your heart and find out if you are healthy. It is a sound amplifier that carries the sound along the pipe to your ears.

240 What's That Noise?

How can sound waves be collected and directed?

Materials
- large piece of paper
- tape
- radio
- friend

STEPS

1. Roll the paper to make one large opening and one small opening. Tape the paper to make a sound funnel.
2. Put the small end of the sound funnel to your ear. (Do not put it in your ear.) What can you hear?
3. Now stand near the radio with the funnel to your ear. What do you notice? Take the funnel away. Is the sound different?
4. Ask your friend to make some soft rustling and moving noises while you hold the funnel to your ear. Can you hear the very soft sounds? (It is important that no loud sounds are put through the sound funnel, as it could damage your hearing.)

Did You Know?
In the past, instead of using hearing aids people who had trouble hearing would use ear trumpets. If someone wanted to say something to them, they would speak into the large end of the ear trumpet. This way they could be heard by the person who had trouble hearing. Today we use hearing aids to help people with hearing.

241 The Matchbox Guitar

How do string instruments work?

STEPS

1. Cut the piece of balsa wood into a flat triangular shape so that its length is a little longer than the width of the matchbox.
2. Place the triangle across the width of the matchbox so that the pointed end is hanging over. You don't need the piece that is hanging over, so cut it off. Now you have what is called the "bridge."
3. Lay the bridge on the closed matchbox and open it up so that it is about three-quarters open.
4. Put the rubber bands over the matchbox lengthways and space them evenly. Make sure the rubber bands are tight. This can be done by opening the matchbox a little more.
5. Raise your bridge so that it stands up. Play your guitar.

Materials
- empty matchbox
- 4 rubber bands
- small piece of balsa wood
- craft knife

Did You Know?
Traditionally, guitar strings were made from cat intestines. These days they are made from nylon, bronze, and steel.

---

242 Snappy Ruler

See how a simple object can make interesting sounds.

STEPS

1. Take the ruler and place it so that it is half on the table and half off the table.
2. Firmly hold the part of the ruler that is on the table. Use your other hand to pull up on the part of the ruler that is off the table.
3. Let go and listen to the sound. Keep repeating this action. Can you make higher sounds and lower sounds by moving the ruler? Why is this happening?

Materials
- plastic or metal ruler
- table edge

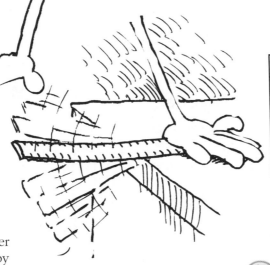

Did You Know?
When an object vibrates through the air, particles bang into each other and sound is produced. Pitch is how high or how low a sound is. When the ruler vibrates at a slower speed, the air particles around it are not as agitated and so the sound is at a lower pitch.

243 Musical Wine Glasses

Find out how sound resonates.

STEPS

1. Put the two glasses on a table.
2. Run your finger around the rim of one of the glasses. What happens?
3. Now, wet your finger with water and run it around the rim of the other glass. You may have to run your finger around it more than once. Keep going until something happens. Can you hear something?
4. Put some water in the glass and repeat step 3.

Materials
- 2 crystal glasses
- water

Did You Know?
Sound has a property called resonance. That means a sound, even if it is soft, when contained in something like glass or wood, bounces off the various surfaces and increases in volume. A guitar sounds as loud as it does because of resonance.

---

244 Making the Distance

Find out how sound waves affect different objects.

Oh great, I think I've made too much noise with my experiment. My friend seems to have left the park altogether!

STEPS

1. Go out to the park.
2. Ask your friend to stand 20 large footsteps away from you. Bang the pan with the spoon.
3. Ask your friend to take 40 more large footsteps away from you. Bang the pan.
4. Keep getting your friend to move back farther. What does your friend notice the farther he or she moves away from you?

Materials
- pan
- large metal spoon
- friend
- park

Did You Know?
Sound travels at a certain speed, which is slower than the speed at which light travels. Sound waves are affected by the quality of the air they are passing through. This is why it is hard to hear in windy weather.

245 Musical Bottles

Find out how differently pitched sounds are made.

Materials
- between 5 and 8 identical bottles
- water
- spoon or fork

STEPS

1. Put the bottles in a line.
2. Add water to the bottles. Fill the first bottle with a little water and the next one with a little more than the first, until you have filled all the bottles with different but increasing amounts of water.
3. Now take the spoon and strike the bottles one after the other.
4. Then strike the bottles in any order. Can you make a tune?

Did You Know?

If you want to make a musical scale, place the bottles in order from the one that makes the lowest sound to the one that makes the highest sound (you might need to add more water to some or tip a little out). See if you can make up a tune, or play one that you know.

DING DING

WHY?

The more water in a bottle the lower the pitch will be. This is because the sound vibrations you can hear come from the actual bottle, and as you add water it takes on a greater vibrating mass. The less water that is in a bottle means there is less weight that vibrates and the pitch is higher.

246 Stickin' to the Outline

Draw an outline of a friend's face using light and shadow.

STEPS

1. Put the chair against a wall.
2. Ask your friend to sit in the chair sideways.
3. Hang the paper on the wall behind your friend's head.
4. Set up the flashlight so that it shines on the paper to make a shadow.
5. Use the marker to trace the outline of your friend's head.

Materials
- bright flashlight
- large piece of stiff paper
- dark room
- friend
- marker
- chair

Did You Know?
This kind of shadow, which shows the outline around an object, is called a silhouette.

247 Standing in the Shadows

Investigate shadows and see how they work.

STEPS

1. Darken the room.
2. Set up the flashlight so that it shines onto the white wall.
3. Invite your two friends to stand in the light. Ask one to stand close to the wall and the other to stand closer to the light. Whose shadow is bigger?
4. Ask them to change positions. What happens to the shadows on the wall? Whose shadow is bigger now? Why do you think this is happening?

Materials
- flashlight
- white wall
- dark room
- 2 friends

Did You Know?
A shadow is made when light cannot pass through an object. The closer the object is to the light, the larger the object becomes.

PHYSICS

PHYSICS: THE SCIENCE DEALING WITH THE PROPERTIES OF MATTER AND ENERGY.

Date:	Experiment:	Notes:

248 Reverse

How do mirrors reflect light?

STEPS

1. Write your name in large letters on a sheet of paper.

2. Now place the mirror upright on the edge of the paper so that you can see your writing reflected. How do the letters look in the mirror? Do any of them look the same in the mirror as they do on the paper?

3. With another sheet of paper, try to write your name in reverse. Hold up the mirror and check your writing. Does it look the right way around? Keep improving your reverse writing to see if you can make the writing in the mirror look the right way around.

Materials
- small rectangular mirror
- sheets of paper
- markers

Did You Know?
Emergency services such as the ambulance use this idea. The word AMBULANCE is written in reverse on the front of an ambulance vehicle so that drivers can read it correctly in their rear view mirrors while driving.

249 Need Your Lenses Fixed?

Demonstrate how lenses work.

STEPS

1. Take your magnifying glass and stand with your back to a bright window.

2. Hold the paper in your other hand. Hold the magnifying glass up so that the light from the window shines onto the paper. What can you see on the paper?

Materials
- magnifying glass
- piece of white paper
- window

Did You Know?
This experiment is demonstrating a lens. A lens is a curved piece of glass. Convex lenses are curved inward and concave lenses are curved outward. When you look in a camera you see a small image. This is because there is a lens in the camera.

250 Rainbow Light

Observe diffraction of light with sunlight.

STEPS

1. Early on a clear and bright sunny morning, set up the box about 4 yd (3.5 m) away from a window with strong sunlight.

2. Fill the glass with water and place it on the box.

3. Look down on the floor for a rainbow. Move the paper around on the floor to capture the rainbow. What colors can you see? How long will this rainbow last?

Materials
- clear drinking glass
- large sheet of paper
- box about 20 in (50 cm) high
- sunny window
- water

Did You Know?
There are many folk stories about rainbows, including the idea that there is a pot of gold at the end of the rainbow. A rainbow is made up of water and light, so a person cannot go under a rainbow or stand at the end of one.

251 Ceiling Rainbows

See how rainbows are made.

STEPS

1. Darken a room.

2. Switch on the flashlight and place the cup on top of the flashlight.

3. Gently pour the water into the cup and watch the ceiling for rainbows.

4. Now do the same with the square container.

5. What kind of rainbows did you see? Did you notice any difference when using the different containers?

Materials
- flashlight
- clear plastic cup
- clear square container
- water in a jug

Did You Know?
The rainbow shape is determined by the container shape. The water creates a prism through which the light travels. Raindrops are also prisms that create rainbows.

252 Color Your Life

Find out how primary colors make secondary colors.

Materials
- flashlight
- red, blue, and yellow cellophane

STEPS

1. Shine the flashlight onto a white wall.
2. Cover the flashlight with red cellophane. Now cover the flashlight with yellow cellophane. What color is made on the wall?
3. Now cover the red cellophane with the blue cellophane. What color is made on the wall?
4. Cover the flashlight with blue cellophane. Now cover the flashlight with yellow cellophane. What color is made on the wall?
5. What other colors can you make using the cellophane? Can you make black?

Did You Know?
Red, yellow, and blue are called the primary colors of light. When combinations of these colors are put together they make secondary colors, such as green, purple, and orange.

253 Mighty Whites

See how white light is made.

Materials
- 3 flashlights
- red, blue, and green cellophane
- tape

STEPS

1. Attach each cellophane color over the light of each flashlight.
2. Turn on the flashlights.
3. Place the flashlights about 4 in (10 cm) apart on a table and shine them at a white wall.
4. Arrange the flashlights so that the light from each flashlight overlaps with the other flashlights.
5. What can you see on the wall?

Did You Know?
You can see a white center and three surrounding colors. The pinkish color that is produced when the blue overlaps the red is called magenta. The color that is produced when the green overlaps the blue is cyan. What other color is there?

254 Am I Upside Down?

See how light is reflected off different surfaces.

Materials
- shiny spoon

STEPS

1. Hold the spoon up to your face with the inward curve pointing away from you.
2. Move it away from your face. How does your face change? Does it change as you expected?
3. Now turn the spoon around. What do you see? Do you see what you expected?

Did You Know?
The magical mirrors that you see at amusement parks work by turning light in different directions.

255 I've Found It!

Investigate the bending of light. This is called refraction.

Materials
- bowl
- friend
- a coin

STEPS

1. Place the bowl on the table.
2. Put the coin in the bowl and stand aside. Can you see the coin?
3. Ask your friend to fill the bowl with water while you are standing to the side.
4. What happens? Can you see the coin now?

Did You Know?
An image of the coin is visible because light rays refract to create an illusion.

256 Rainbow in Your Hand

Observe different prisms that can create rainbows.

STEPS

1. Pour the water into the pan.
2. Place the mirror against the side of the pan.
3. Place your hand in front of the mirror but not in front of the sunlight.
4. Where is the rainbow reflected? What is creating the prism for the light to travel through?

Materials
- shallow pan
- small mirror
- water
- strong sunlight

Did You Know?
Ray is the word used for the stream of light seen on your hand. When rays of light pass through prisms, they create rainbows. This is called diffraction.

---

257 Filter Fun

See the effect of colored light on objects of different colors.

STEPS

1. Tape the piece of red cellophane over the flashlight. Now shine the flashlight on the different colored objects. What happens?
2. Take off the red cellophane and tape the piece of blue cellophane over the flashlight. Now shine the flashlight on the different colored objects. What happens?
3. Take off the blue cellophane and tape the piece of green cellophane over the flashlight. Now shine the flashlight on the different colored objects. What happens?

Materials
- flashlight
- red, green, and blue cellophane
- objects of different colors, especially red, green, and blue
- tape

Did You Know?
When light hits a colored object some of the light is absorbed and some reflected. The color that you see is the color that is reflected. Some objects look black because they absorb all the light that shines on them. Tiny dots of these three colors moving very fast on your TV screen make the colored images that you watch.

258 Turning to White

See how white is made up of many colors.

STEPS

1. Draw a circle with the compass on the cardboard. Cut out the circle.
2. Use the protractor to mark out six equal sections.
3. Shade in each section with the following colors—red, blue, green, yellow, orange, and violet.
4. Push the pencil through the center of the circle so that you can spin it like a top. Spin the circle. What happens?

Materials
- colored pencils
- piece of white cardboard
- compass
- protractor
- pencil
- scissors

Did You Know?
Isaac Newton discovered that white light was made up of many colors by shining white light through a prism.

259 Combing the Shadows

Look at an aspect of sunlight.

STEPS

1. Find a clear window with sunlight shining through.
2. On a flat surface hold the comb upright in the sunlight so it makes a shadow.
3. Incline the comb away from the Sun. What happens to the shadow? What kind of shadow is made by the Sun?

Materials
- comb

Did You Know?
Some light rays fan out but the Sun's rays hit Earth at a parallel angle, making shadows that are straight.

260 Who's Got the Fastest Car?

See the effects of friction on different surfaces.

"Hey, go easy on the wheels. That's sandpaper we are driving on."

STEPS

1. Take the toy car and push it along the surface of the wood.
2. Now push the toy car along the strip of sandpaper.
3. Now push the toy car along the carpet. On which surface does your car run the smoothest?

Did You Know?

Cars skid on wet roads because the water on the surface creates less friction between the wheels and the road. The treads on your car's tires help solve this problem. The water is forced into the spaces between the treads and the tire surface stays on the road. "Bald" tires are not safe. Inspect your family car's tires and see how the water is moved out of the way.

Materials
- long strip of sandpaper
- long, smooth piece of wood
- long stretch of smooth carpet
- small toy car

---

261 Which Parachute?

How do different materials affect air resistance?

STEPS

1. Take the plastic bag and cut it into a 12 in (30 cm) square. Tie four pieces of string to each corner of the square. Attach the string to a large blob of clay.
2. Take the handkerchief and tie four pieces of string, one to each corner. Attach the string to a large blob of clay.
3. Take the paper, punch a hole in each corner, and tie four pieces of string to each corner. Attach the string to a large blob of clay.
4. Stand on a chair and drop each parachute. Record the times for each parachute from letting go until it hits the ground.

Did You Know?

Very strong nylon fabric makes the best parachute material because it is light and flexible. The material that makes up the top of the parachute is called the canopy.

Materials
- plastic bag
- 12 pieces of string, each 14 in (35 cm) long
- modeling clay
- handkerchief
- piece of paper, the same size as the handkerchief
- scissors
- hole punch
- stopwatch

262 Watch This!

Demonstrate the quality of inertia (keeping still, unless something is pushing or pulling you).

Materials
- a piece of cloth with no hems to cover a table with straight edges
- heavy spoons, forks, and knives
- plates and cups with smooth bases
- table on a carpeted floor

STEPS

1. Lay the cloth on the table.
2. Set the table with the utensils, plates, and cups close to the edge of the cloth.
3. Hold the cloth with two hands and pull quickly down and away. Keep the cloth parallel and don't pull one side more than another.
4. Keep trying until you get the cloth out without disturbing the objects. Try adding more objects after this.

Did You Know?
Isaac Newton investigated the qualities of inertia and found that objects must have force applied to them to move. The objects on the table don't move because the force is not acting on the objects but rather on the cloth.

---

263 Unusual Pendulum

See how a pendulum moves.

Materials
- string
- modeling clay
- sunglasses
- friend

STEPS

1. Attach the string to a large blob of the clay.
2. Hold the string in your hand and let the pendulum swing.
3. Ask your friend to hold the sunglasses over their right eye. Ask them to tell you what is happening.
4. Now ask your friend to hold the sunglasses over their left eye. Ask them to tell you what is happening.

Did You Know?
This is an illusion. Did you notice that when the sunglasses are held over the left eye the pendulum appears to be moving in a clockwise direction, and opposite for the right eye?

264 Turning Inside a Balloon

Find out how an object turns within a confined space.

Materials
- clear balloon
- small coin

STEPS

1. Place the coin inside the balloon and blow the balloon up. Be careful not to overblow the balloon and make it too stretched. Tie the end of the balloon.
2. Hold the tied end of the balloon like a bowling ball.
3. Start to turn the balloon around quickly in a circle.
4. Once you feel the coin starting to move around in a circular path, hold the balloon still and let the coin keep moving. Why do you think this is happening? Why does the coin have this kind of path?

Did You Know?
The spinning coin is like a spinning top. A spinning top stays upright because of the forces of energy that keep it there. The same effect is happening with the coin inside the balloon. An inward force is making it travel in a circular way.

265 Sailing the High Seas

See how the shape of objects helps them float.

Materials
- modeling clay
- bucket
- water

STEPS

1. Fill the bucket with water.
2. Take the clay and shape it into a ball. Put the clay in the water. What happens?
3. Take the clay and make it into the shape of a bowl. Put it into the water. What happens?

Did You Know?
Whether an object will float or not depends on how dense it is. Ships float because, even though they are heavy, they have less density than water.

266 Will Humpty-Dumpty Crack?

How strong is an eggshell?

STEPS

1. Wrap a strip of masking tape around the middle of each egg. Keep a gap between the ends of the masking tape.
2. Carefully make a hole in each eggshell between the gap in the tape.
3. Empty the contents of the eggs into a cup.
4. Put the end of the scissors into the hole and cut around the middle of the eggshell covered with the masking tape. Separate the halves and trim off any jagged pieces of shell.
5. Place the half-eggshells dome-side up on a flat surface so that they make a square.
6. Lay the square of cardboard on the eggshells.
7. Stand a large can gently on top of the cardboard.
8. Keep stacking on the cans one at a time. How many cans were you able to stack before any of the eggshells cracked?
9. Weigh the cans on the kitchen scales and work out the weight supported by the eggshells.

Materials
- two eggs
- masking tape
- fingernail scissors
- large can of food and other smaller cans of food
- square of rigid cardboard
- kitchen scales

WHY?

The hardest natural substance on Earth is a diamond. It is made from layers of compacted carbon and can only be scratched by other diamonds. Diamonds form by carbon being exposed to high temperatures and pressures for millions of years deep underground. They are very valuable.

Did You Know?

The strength of the egg is in its dome shape. No single point of the dome supports the whole weight of the cans on top of it. The weight spreads along the curved walls to the wide base, allowing the eggshell to hold more weight. This fact is valuable for architects.

267 Funny Funnel

See the effects of changes in air pressure.

Materials
- funnel
- piece of cardboard the size of a postcard

STEPS

1. Place the cardboard on the table.
2. Hold the funnel close to the cardboard with the small end pointing upward.
3. Use your mouth to suck air through the funnel.
4. With the funnel in the same position, blow hard. What happens?

Did You Know?

Air pressure presses on our bodies, but we don't feel it because our bodies press back with equal force.

268 Fun to Spin

See how designed objects can move through the air.

Materials
- paper (normal weight), thin paper, and thick cardboard
- ruler
- scissors

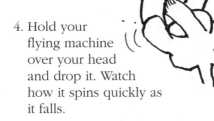

STEPS

1. Take the normal weight paper and make a strip of paper 8 in (20 cm) long and ¾ in (2 cm) wide.
2. Measure ⅝ in (1.5 cm) from each end and make a cut halfway across the strip. The cuts should be on opposite sides of the strip.
3. Turn the paper strip and use the cuts near the ends to make a closed shape. The shape should hold together and not undo.
4. Hold your flying machine over your head and drop it. Watch how it spins quickly as it falls.
5. Make another fun spinner with the thin paper then the thick cardboard. What happens?

Did You Know?

Aerodynamics is the word used for understanding how objects move through air. This study includes kites, planes, paper planes, rockets, and how objects like balls move through the air.

269 Feeling a Little Tense?

See how some objects float some of the time.

STEPS

1. Fill the bucket with water.
2. Gently place the lid upside down in the water. Does it float?
3. Now turn the lid the other way and place it gently in the water. What happens now? Does it float?
4. Now place the lid gently sideways into the water. Can you get it to float?

Materials
- metal lid from a jar
- bucket
- water

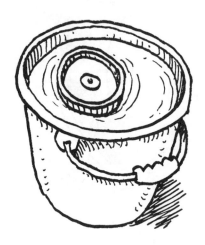

Did You Know?
Water has a quality called surface tension. This means it can keep some objects afloat when placed in a certain way on the water. Some insects can stand on water because of surface tension.

270 Feelin' the Pressure

See how air pressure works.

STEPS

1. Fill the glass to the top with water.
2. Take the cardboard and put it on top.
3. Warning! Do the rest of this experiment over the sink.
4. Holding the cardboard in place, turn the glass upside down.
5. Now take your hand away from the cardboard. What happens?

Materials
- drinking glass
- water
- piece of cardboard the size of a postcard

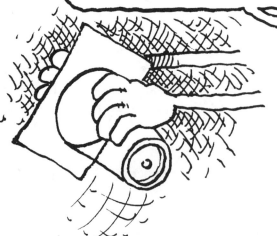

I am doing this experiment over the sink.

Did You Know?
Air has a quality called pressure. This is a force that pushes in all directions, even upward.

271 Falling Over

Show how energy can be transferred from one object to another.

Materials
- 2 packs of dominoes
- large flat area, e.g. table

STEPS

1. Stand the dominoes up on end in a line on the table.
2. Set the dominoes about ¾ in (2 cm) apart.
3. Tap the first domino and watch what happens.

Did You Know?
This is called the domino effect. This term is used to describe how one action can cause a chain of events. This can be seen in storms when trees fall.

272 Crater Than Thou

See the effect of falling objects.

Materials
- large bowl
- flour
- large marble
- small marble
- tennis ball

STEPS

1. Fill the bowl with flour and pat it down gently. Make it smooth on top.
2. From a height, drop a large marble into the middle of the flour. What do you notice?
3. Now smooth the flour again and repeat step 2 with a smaller marble. What do you notice?
4. Now smooth the flour again and repeat step 2 with a tennis ball. What do you notice?

Did You Know?
Craters are formed in a similar way to this experiment. The larger the object, the greater the force with which it hits Earth and the larger the crater it forms. When asteroids hit Earth, they act in the same way as the marble did in the flour.

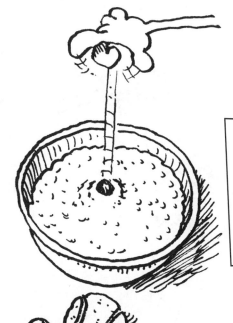

273 Catch Me, I'm Falling!

See how air resistance affects different objects.

STEPS

1. One by one, drop all the objects except for the tissue paper. Which one is quickest to hit the ground?
2. Now take the tissue paper. Scrunch up one of the sheets.
3. Stand on a chair and drop both sheets of tissue paper. Which one hits the ground first?

Materials
- sheet of paper
- feather
- leaf
- book
- 2 pieces of tissue paper

Did You Know?
High-speed drag-race cars are designed the way they are to reduce the amount of air resistance. The less resistance, the faster they will go.

274 Bounce!

See how energy is transferred by bouncing balls of different sizes.

STEPS

1. Bounce the basketball and take note of how high it bounces.
2. Bounce the tennis ball from the same height as the basketball and take note of how high it bounces.
3. Now hold the tennis ball on top of the basketball. What do you think will happen when you drop them? Which one will bounce the highest?
4. Ask your friend to watch and then drop the balls. What happens?

Materials
- basketball
- tennis ball
- friend
- large outdoor area

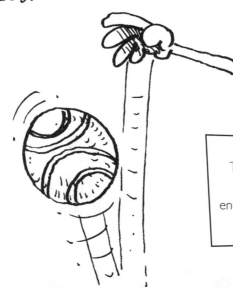

Did You Know?
The tennis ball bounces much higher than the basketball. This is because energy from the basketball is transferred to the tennis ball.

275 Bounce Higher!

Investigate bouncing energy.

STEPS

1. Use the tape measure to measure 16 in (40 cm), 32 in (80 cm), and 48 in (120 cm) on a wall. Mark these with masking tape.
2. Drop a tennis ball from the 16 in (40 cm) height and ask your friend to watch what happens. How high did the ball bounce? Do this two more times and record how high it bounces each time.
3. Do the same using the height of 32 in (80 cm).
4. Repeat the experiment at the 48 in (120 cm) height. Why do you think the ball bounces at different heights?

Materials
- 3 tennis balls
- tape measure
- chair
- outside space with a hard ground surface
- masking tape
- friend

Did You Know?
When a ball is bounced it conserves its energy. That is why it bounces up close to the height from which it was dropped.

---

276 Bounce Factors

How do different surfaces affect the bounce of balls?

STEPS

1. In the hard floor area bounce the basketball and then bounce the tennis ball. What happens?
2. Now go to a carpeted area and bounce the basketball and the tennis ball. What happens? Why do you think the balls bounced differently in the different places?

I think I know now why my Mom didn't let us bounce our ball on the carpet. Because it doesn't bounce very well.

Materials
- basketball
- tennis ball
- carpeted floor area
- hard floor area

Did You Know?
When a ball is falling it still maintains the energy it starts with. When it hits a soft surface like carpet, some of the ball's energy is absorbed into the carpet because it is spongier. When a ball hits a hard surface it only loses a very small amount of its energy.

277 How to Make a Parachute

See the way pressure affects falling objects.

STEPS

1. Take the plastic bag and cut it into a 12 in (30 cm) square.
2. Tie the string to each corner of the square.
3. Tie the other ends of the string to the spoon.
4. Stand on a chair and drop the parachute. What happens?

Materials
- plastic bag
- 4 pieces of string, each 14 in (35 cm) long
- spoon
- scissors

I don't know if I would trust this to jump out of a plane with. But it seems to work!

Did You Know?
To make parachutes easier to control, a hole is made in the top. This hole lessens the air resistance.

278 The Swing of Things

Demonstrate that for every action there needs to be an equal and opposite reaction.

STEPS

1. Place yourself comfortably in the chair.
2. Without letting your feet touch the ground, see if you can move yourself. Can you move yourself as easily as you thought you could?

Materials
- chair with wheels, e.g. a swivel chair
- space

Did You Know?
It is difficult to move because you are not pushing against anything. The wheels on the chair cause your pushing energy to go into the air. If you pushed against something solid, you would move because the solid object would not move back.

279 Hangin' Out For Answers

See how weights can balance each other.

STEPS

1. Take one of the plastic containers and tie a piece of string to each side.
2. Repeat with the other container.
3. Attach one container to each end of the coat hanger.
4. Now hang the coat hanger from a table or ledge so that it can move freely.
5. Put various objects into the containers. What happens?
6. Can you get two containers to hang at the same level?

Materials
- coat hanger
- 2 empty plastic containers of the same type
- 4 pieces of string 8 in (20 cm) in length
- household objects, e.g. pencil, eraser, sharpener, fork, spoon etc.

Did You Know?
The force pulling down on an object is called gravity. We walk on the Earth because of gravity. Without gravity people would float off into space.

280 Making a Siphon

Find out how water pressure works by making a siphon.

STEPS

1. Fill one soft drink bottle with water and put one end of the hose into it.
2. Use your mouth to suck the other end of the hose until water comes through. Don't drink the water.
3. Quickly put your thumb over the end.
4. Now raise the full soft drink bottle so that it is higher than the empty soft drink bottle.
5. Put the end of the hose you are holding into the empty soft drink bottle. What do you notice?

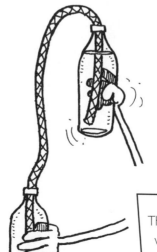

Materials
- 2 empty soft drink bottles with openings big enough for a garden hose
- clean piece of garden hose about 24-32 in (60-80 cm) long
- water

Did You Know?
This experiment shows how water pressure works. In your home, water comes out of the faucets because of water pressure.

281 My Own Plane Wing

See how wing design works.

STEPS

1. Measure 4 in (10 cm) from one end of the paper on each of the long sides. Draw a line across the width.
2. Take the other end of the paper and fold it over to the drawn line. Don't crease the paper.
3. Hold your thumb over the end while you tape it in that position.
4. Gently press a bamboo skewer through both layers of paper at the center approximately 1½ in (4 cm) in from the fold. Take the skewer out.
5. Thread the string through the holes. Ask your friend to hold both ends of the string tight.
6. Blow on the fold of the paper from the front. Can you get the paper to rise up the string?

Materials
- piece of paper 6 in × 20 in (15 cm × 50 cm)
- tape
- bamboo skewer
- length of string 8 in (20 cm) long
- friend
- ruler
- pencil

Did You Know?
This is the same design as a plane wing. When planes fly, they rush forward at a high speed and the wind rushing over the wings helps the plane to rise.

282 Magic Floating Objects

Show how an object travels in the air.

Did You Know?
The air flows around the balls evenly and while the pull of gravity draws the balls downward, the air pressure pushes the balls up. The objects can float because the forces on them are equal. This is how planes fly! Wings on planes are designed to have less pressure on the top of the wings than under the wings. This is how planes stay up and seem to defy gravity.

Materials
- hair dryer
- light balls, e.g. table tennis (ping pong) balls or balloons
- toilet roll or kitchen foil roll

STEPS

1. Turn the hair dryer on high and turn it upward so that the air is shooting straight up.
2. Put the balloon or table tennis ball in the stream of air. Hold the hair dryer as still as you can.
3. Watch the objects floating in the air.
4. Try tilting the hair dryer to each side. What happens?
5. Add more objects. How many can you have floating at one time?
6. Put the toilet roll over the stream of air so that the air is funneled. What happens to the floating balls now? What is happening?

283 Lost My Marbles

Show how pushing and pulling can make objects move or stop.

STEPS

1. Tape the cardboard lid to the skateboard.
2. Put the marbles in the lid so that they are not close to each other.
3. Give the skateboard a gentle push. What is happening to the marbles?
4. Stop the skateboard by pulling it back. What is happening now?

Materials
- marbles of different sizes
- tape
- cardboard lid
- skateboard

Did You Know?
Once you start an object moving it will keep going by itself until it is stopped by something. This is called inertia. Have you noticed that you are pushed forward in your seat when a car stops suddenly? What is acting on you is inertia.

---

284 Lifting Higher

See how sideways force affects objects.

STEPS

1. Cut a piece of string about 3 ft (1 m) long.
2. Attach the string to the table tennis ball with tape.
3. Stand in an open, outdoor space and start to spin the string around your head. Keep turning it for a short time. What is happening to the string and the table tennis ball? Can you feel any pull on the string?

Materials
- table tennis (ping pong) ball
- string
- tape
- scissors
- tape measure

Did You Know?
This sideways force is called centrifugal force. This force is working against gravity and stops the table tennis ball from falling to the ground. Spinning rides at amusement parks use centrifugal force to keep people up off the ground.

285 The Boxing Kangaroos

See how heat rises and that it is a force.

STEPS

1. Draw four kangaroos on the cardboard and cut them out.
2. Take the bamboo skewers and make a cross. Tape them together in the middle.
3. Cut four equal lengths of string about 4–6 in (10–15 cm). Attach each kangaroo to a piece of string with tape. Then tie the other end of the string on each of the bamboo arms.
4. Cut a length of string about 4 in (10 cm) long and attach one end to the ruler and tie the other end to the middle of the bamboo sticks.
5. Hold the mobile over a radiator in your home. Can you see evidence of the way the air is moving?

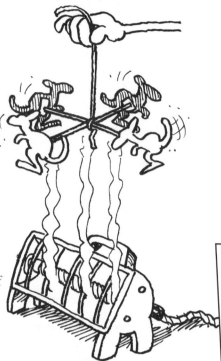

Materials
- large piece of thin cardboard
- ruler
- 2 bamboo skewers
- string
- tape
- pencil
- scissors
- oil radiator

Did You Know?
Electricity is produced by a similar method. Coal is burned, which heats water. The heated water creates steam and heat, which turns huge turbines and by farther process produces electricity.

286 Melting Ice Hands-free

See how light is intensified through a magnifying glass.

STEPS

1. Take two pieces of ice straight from the freezer. Put each of them in a shallow bowl. Place the bowls in the sunlight.
2. Take the magnifying glass. Hold it up so that it catches the sunlight. If you hold it correctly it should make a beam of light. Don't put your hand in this beam.
3. Direct the beam onto one of the ice cubes. Is it melting more quickly than the other ice cube?

Materials
- direct sunlight
- magnifying glass
- ice cubes

Did You Know?
When light passes through a magnifying glass it is intensified because of the shape of the glass.

287 Jumping Up

Investigate static electricity.

STEPS

1. Place the candy sprinkles in the plastic container with the lid on.
2. Rub the lid with the cloth to charge it.
3. Carefully rub your finger across the top of the lid.
4. Do the candy sprinkles stay up or fall down? What can you observe?

Materials
- candy sprinkles
- small plastic container with a lid
- cloth made of wool

Did You Know?

Charged sprinkles fall down or are repelled. Sprinkles that are neutral stay attached to the lid.

288 Seeing Ions in Action

Can you make pieces of paper stick to a balloon?

STEPS

1. Blow up your balloon to a size that will still fit in your hand. Tie it.
2. Use the hole punch to cut a small circle in your paper.
3. Rub the balloon on your hair about 12 times. Don't press too hard and make sure that your hair is clean.
4. Hold the balloon close to the paper and see what happens.

Materials
- balloon
- paper
- hole punch

Did You Know?

An ion is a group of atoms that become electrically charged by gaining or losing an electron. Have you heard that opposites attract? Your balloon has stolen electrons from your hair and this gives it a negative charge. The paper has lost electrons so it has a positive charge. When they meet they are attracted to each other!

289 Like Them Lemons?

Make a battery.

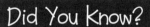

Did You Know?
Thomas Edison (1847–1931) invented the first light bulb.

Materials
- 2 lemons
- 2 flat strips of zinc
- 2 flat strips of copper
- 9-volt light bulb
- insulated wire
- pliers

STEPS

1. Put a lemon on the table and place a strip of copper in one end and a strip of zinc in the other. The strips should be parallel to each other.
2. Repeat this for the other lemon.
3. Take the insulated wire and cut off two pieces 8 in (20 cm) long. Take one of the pieces and cut it in half. Trim the plastic insulation from the ends of the wire so that there is some wire visible.
4. Take the long piece of wire, attach it to one of the points of the light bulb, and attach the other end to one of the pieces of zinc on one of the lemons.
5. With the shorter piece of wire, connect the piece of copper on the same lemon to the zinc on the other lemon.
6. Holding the last piece of wire on the insulated section, connect one end to the final piece of copper. Connect the other end to the other point on the light bulb.

290 Double Balloon Static

Make static electricity and show electricity attracting and repelling.

Materials
- balloons
- string
- sweater (preferably wool)
- thick paper

STEPS

1. Blow up the balloons and tie the ends.
2. Attach the string to the ends of the balloons.
3. Rub the balloons on the sweater.
4. Hold them up by the string. What happens?
5. Now place the paper between the balloons. What happens now?

Did You Know?
Electricity can repel, which means to push away. When the two balloons are charged they repel each other. The paper attracts the balloons.

291 Don't Sink the Boat

Investigate the energy of static electricity.

STEPS

1. Use the corks as boats and place them in the tray of water. Push them under the water so that they are wet.
2. Rub the pen on your clothing quickly.
3. Use the pen to drag the boats across the water. Be careful not to touch the water or the cork with the pen. If this happens recharge the pen by rubbing it on your clothes again.

Materials
- corks
- plastic pens
- shallow tray
- water
- cloth (preferably wool)

Did You Know?
Lightning is a very strong form of static electricity. No one knows how it is formed.

292 Balloon Static

Make static electricity.

STEPS

1. Tear the paper into small pieces and put them on the table.
2. Blow up the balloon and tie the end.
3. Rub the balloon on the sweater.
4. What happens when you hold the balloon on the wall in a warm, dry room?
5. What happens when you hold the balloon near running water?
6. What happens when you hold the balloon over the torn pieces of paper?

Materials
- balloons
- water faucet
- sweater (preferably wool)
- paper

Did You Know?
Everything around us is made up of tiny little parts called atoms, and atoms are made of even smaller parts, which are called protons, electrons, and neutrons. The protons, electrons, and neutrons are very different. Protons have a positive (+) charge. Electrons have a negative (−) charge. Neutrons have no charge. Usually, atoms have the same number of electrons and protons. When the atom has no charge, it is "neutral." If you rub things together, electrons can move from one atom to another, then some atoms get extra electrons and the other atoms might have a negative charge or no charge at all. When charges are separated like this, it is called static electricity.

293 My Magnetic House

Discover everyday magnetic objects.

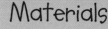

STEPS

1. Arrange your testing items into two groups: items that you think are magnetic and those you think are not magnetic.
2. Test the items. If the magnet attaches to the object, it is magnetic.
3. Write a list of the items that are magnetic.

Materials
- any items around your house such as forks, spoons, paper clips, kitchen foil, pencil, toy cars, soft toys
- magnet

Did You Know?
There are five planets with magnetic fields in our solar system. They are Earth, Neptune, Jupiter, Uranus, and Saturn.

---

294 Slippery Snake

See how magnets work through glass.

STEPS

1. Use the clay to make a snake about 2–2½ in (5–6 cm) long.
2. Place two paperclips, one on top of the other, into the back of the snake.
3. Place the snake in the glass jar so that the paperclips are close to the inside wall of the jar.
4. Make your snake slither by holding the magnet on the outside of the jar and moving the magnet up and down.
5. What is happening?

Materials
- paperclips
- modeling clay
- large glass jar
- magnets

Did You Know?
Magnets have two poles, a north and south pole. Each pole is on the end of the magnet.

295 Opposites Attract

Find out how magnetic poles attract and repel.

STEPS

1. Fill the tray with water.
2. Attach the magnets to the top of the toy boats.
3. Put the boats on the water and push them toward one another.
4. What happens when opposite poles on the boats are close to each other? Do the boats come together or pull apart? Try this with the same poles close to each other. Do the boats come together or pull apart?

Materials
- toy boats
- straight magnets with north and south marked on them
- tape
- shallow tray
- water

Did You Know?
There is a difference between the geographic North Pole and the magnetic north pole of Earth. The magnetic north pole of Earth is moving at a rate of approximately 25 miles (40 km) a year.

---

296 North Pole or South Pole?

Discover the poles of magnets.

STEPS

1. Put the string around the center of the magnet.
2. Attach the string to a table or ledge.
3. When the magnet is still, use the compass to find out which way is north.
4. Mark the north pole "N" and the south pole "S" on the magnet.

Materials
- compass
- string
- tape
- straight magnets
- marker

Did You Know?
The magnetism is strongest in the poles of magnets. The poles react differently when the same poles are together and when opposite poles are placed together.

297 Matchbox Cars

Show how magnets work through solid objects.

STEPS

1. Decorate the matchboxes to make them into race cars.
2. Tape a paperclip inside each box.
3. Make the piece of cardboard into a racetrack for two cars.
4. Attach a magnet to the stick.
5. Lift the racetrack off the table by resting it on two stacks of books.
6. Move the magnet under the cardboard to make the race cars on top of the cardboard racetrack move.
7. Make another stick with a magnet so a friend can play with you.

Did You Know?
Magnets are very strong and can ruin watches, clocks, computer disks, television screens, and videotapes if they are placed too close.

Materials
- paperclips
- empty matchboxes
- colored pencils or markers
- stick about 12 in (20 cm) long
- magnets
- rectangular piece of thick cardboard
- tape
- 2 stacks of books

298 A Magnet Can be a Compass

Make a magnet into a compass, indicating a north–south direction.

STEPS

1. Roll the clay into a ball. Flatten one side to make a cone shape.
2. Push the eraser end of the pencil into the clay so the pencil is vertical and secure.
3. Carefully balance the horseshoe magnet on the point of the pencil.
4. Watch the magnet slowly move to a north–south direction.

Materials
- modeling clay
- sharp pencil with an eraser at the other end
- Horseshoe magnet

Did You Know?
The Earth has a magnetic force that is strong enough to attract your magnet and move it to swing in a north–south direction.

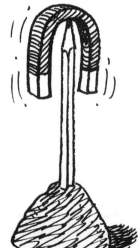

299 Magnetic Field

Demonstrate a magnetic field.

Materials
- iron filings
- paper
- magnets

STEPS

1. Place the magnet on the table with the paper placed on top.
2. Put the iron filings on the paper.
3. Move the paper over the magnet and see what happens.

Did You Know?

People have been using magnets as tools for a long time. Magnets were originally known as magnetite and lodestone.

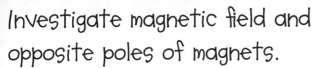

---

300 Double Magnetism

Investigate magnetic field and opposite poles of magnets.

Materials
- iron filings
- paper
- pencil
- magnets

STEPS

1. Place the magnets on the table with the opposite poles about 2 in (5 cm) apart.
2. Place the paper on top and gently scatter the iron filings on top of the paper.
3. Move the paper gently. "Draw" a picture with the iron filings.
4. Try this again with the same poles facing each other. Does the pattern of the iron filings look different?

Did You Know?

Lodestone (a magnet) was very useful to sailors when they needed to navigate. They discovered that when the lodestone was hung on a string, it showed a north–south direction.

301 Demagnetize Me

Show how magnets can destroy magnetic materials.

Materials
- unwanted audio
- cassette tape
- magnet
- tape player

STEPS

1. Play the audio cassette tape. Stop it after a few minutes.
2. Take the audio cassette tape out of the tape player and pull out the brown tape.
3. Wave the magnet closely over the brown tape.
4. Wind the audio tape back into the cassette cover.
5. Play the tape again. What do you notice?

Did You Know?

The magnet has wiped the recording on the audio cassette tape. These tapes are called magnetic tapes. This means the sound that you hear is stored on the tape by small magnetic particles. The magnet used in this experiment is more powerful than the magnetic particles of the tape and therefore destroys the stored information.

302 The Amazing Jumping Men

See the relationship between electricity and magnets.

Materials
- large long screw
- insulated wire
- C-cell battery
- pliers
- box of paperclips
- lightweight paper
- scissors
- pens

Did You Know?

Electromagnets are different than other magnets because the magnetic force is created by the electric current. If the electric current is taken away, it stops the metal from being magnetic.

STEPS

1. Draw some small people on the paper. Cut them out and attach a paperclip to each one.
2. Cut a piece of insulation wire and strip about 6 in (15 cm) of insulation from the wire. Twist the exposed wires into one.
3. Wrap the wire around the screw 10–15 times.
4. Connect the two ends of the wire to the two ends of the battery. Now you have made an electromagnet.
5. See if you can get the paperclips to attach to your electromagnet.

303 Measuring Temperature

Make a device that measures temperature.

STEPS

1. Fill the bottle until it is three-quarters full of cold water.
2. Add a few drops of the food dye.
3. Put the straw into the bottle so that it goes into the water.
4. Use the clay to secure the straw in the bottle. Make sure it is airtight.
5. Tape the piece of cardboard to the straw using two pieces of tape, one at the bottom and one at the top.
6. Suck the straw gently until the water rises to about halfway.
7. Use a marker to mark the water level in the straw on the cardboard.
8. Put the bottle in a warm place; the water will rise.
9. Use a different colored marker and mark where the water has risen on the cardboard.
10. Now put the bottle in the refrigerator. The water level goes down when the temperature gets cooler.
11. Use a different colored marker and mark where the water level is on the cardboard.

Materials
- food dye
- clear bottle
- markers
- cold water
- modeling clay
- piece of cardboard
- tape
- drinking straw

Did You Know?
The device for measuring temperature is called a thermometer.

304 Catching Rain Drops

Observe the differences in the size of rain drops.

STEPS

1. Secure the tissue paper with the paperclips on top of the cardboard.
2. Carefully drip some rain drops onto the tissue paper and let the water seep through to the cardboard.
3. Let the cardboard and tissue paper dry.
4. Take the paperclips off and take off the tissue paper.
5. The cardboard will now be covered with different-sized colorful rain drops.

Materials
- colored tissue paper
- paperclips
- white cardboard
- eye dropper
- water

Did You Know?
Every rain drop is made up of more than a million tiny droplets of water!

305 The Shape of Rain Drops

See the shape of rain drops when they land.

STEPS

1. Fill the eye dropper with clean water.
2. Hold the dropper about 12 in (30 cm) above the paper and drip one drop of water on the paper.
3. Trace around the edge of the drop with the marker or pen.
4. Repeat steps 1, 2, and 3. Are they the same shape?

Materials
- eye dropper (to act as rain)
- marker or pen
- paper

Did You Know?
H_2O is the scientific name for water.

306 Freezing Cold—Part A

How long does it take for water to freeze?

Materials
- clock
- small plastic toy (optional)
- clear plastic cup

STEPS

1. Fill the plastic cup with water and put the plastic toy in the cup.
2. Place the plastic cup in the freezer.
3. Start timing! Check the cup at half-hour intervals until the water has frozen. (This may take a few hours.)
4. Record what you see each half hour.

I just knew I should have put on something warmer when I got out of the toy box this morning!

Did You Know?

Ice is a solid. When you heat ice its molecules move really fast and that is how the ice melts to become a liquid.

---

307 Freezing Cold—Part B

How long does it take for ice to melt?

Materials
- clock
- plastic toy in ice (see Experiment 306)
- tray

STEPS

1. Using the frozen plastic toy from Experiment 306, place it upside down on the tray.
2. Start timing how long it will take the ice to melt. Check the cup at half-hour intervals until the ice has melted. (This may take a few hours.)
3. Record what you see each half hour. Which one took longer—the ice to melt, or the water to freeze?

How long is it going to take me to thaw? All of my blood is going to my head!

Did You Know?

The warmer the air, the faster the molecules in the air will move. The faster the molecules in the air move, the faster ice will melt!

308 Living in Ice

Observe the effects salt has on ice.

Materials
- lots of ice cubes
- salt shaker with salt

STEPS

1. Use the ice cubes to build an igloo (or a square shaped house). You will notice the difference between building with blocks and building with ice.
2. Sprinkle the ice with salt. Has this made a difference to your building?

Did You Know?
Salt helps ice stick together!

---

309 Melting Salty Ice

See the difference between melting salty water and non-salty water.

Materials
- clock
- salty ice cubes (to be made the night before by mixing salt into warm water, pouring it into an ice cube tray and placing it in the freezer)
- non-salty ice cubes
- 2 pieces of paper
- pen

STEPS

1. Write an "S" on a piece of paper to make it easier to identify the salty ice cubes.
2. Place a salty ice cube on the "S" piece of paper.
3. Place a normal ice cube on the other piece of paper.
4. Start timing. Do you think they will melt at the same rate? If not, which one do you think will melt more quickly?

Did You Know?
In places where snow is a problem on roads and driveways during winter, they put salt on snow to make it melt quicker!

WEATHER

WEATHER: THE STATE OF THE ATMOSPHERE AT A PLACE AND A TIME AS REGARDS HEAT, CLOUDINESS, DRYNESS, SUNSHINE, WIND AND RAIN.

Date:	Experiment:	Notes:

310 Make Your Own Thunder

What causes thunder?

Materials
- balloon

STEPS

1. Blow up the balloon.
2. Put a hand on each end of the balloon and push your hands toward each other until the balloon pops.

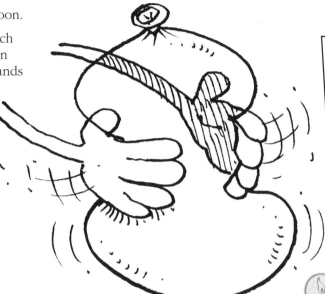

Did You Know?

You create your own thunder because the air inside the balloon moves so fast when you pop the balloon.

311 Make Your Own Lightning

Make your own lightning.

Materials
- comb
- piece of wool
- metal doorknob

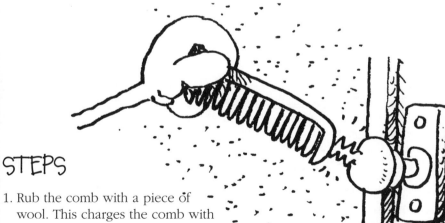

STEPS

1. Rub the comb with a piece of wool. This charges the comb with electricity.
2. Hold the comb near a metal door knob, which is uncharged. You should see a small spark because electricity is jumping from the charged object (the comb) to the neutral object (the doorknob).

Did You Know?

Lightning is a huge electric spark that jumps from the clouds to the ground.

312 Your Own Hurricane!

Experience your own hurricane.

STEPS

1. Spin the piece of string around your head. The toy will feel like it is pulling away from you the faster you spin it around.

Materials
- a piece of string, about 40 in (100 cm) long with an object tied securely to the end of it (a soft toy is a good choice)

Did You Know?
When a hurricane occurs, the wind tries to pull away from the middle. When the wind pulls hard enough it makes a wind-free hole in the middle. This is called the eye of the storm.

313 How Heavy is the Air?

See how heavy air can be.

STEPS

1. Tie some string in the middle of the stick and then attach the other end of the string to the bottom of the coat hanger.
2. Hook the coat hanger somewhere so that the stick can swing.
3. Tape some string onto each balloon.
4. Tie the other end of the string from each balloon loosely to one end of each stick.
5. Balance the balloons.
6. Carefully take one of the balloons off the stick and blow the balloon up.
7. Put the blown-up balloon back onto the stick.
8. The stick should be unbalanced. Which end is heavier?

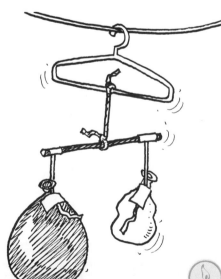

Materials
- 2 balloons
- string
- stick about 8 in (20 cm) long
- a coat hanger

Did You Know?
Air on the top of mountains is very thin and it weighs less than air at sea level!

314 Heat is in the Air

See how much room warm air occupies.

STEPS

1. Ask for help to boil some water in the pan.
2. Stretch the balloon over the opening of the jar.
3. Take the pan off the stove, allow to cool for a few minutes and place the jar in the water. (Caution: If you place a glass jar directly into boiling water it might crack.)
4. Watch for a few minutes and see what happens to the balloon.

Materials
- balloon
- narrow glass jar
- pan
- water

Did You Know?

The air that is inside the balloon gets bigger because the molecules are getting warmer and moving around more quickly.

315 What is the Greenhouse Effect?

Find out about the greenhouse effect.

STEPS

1. Put one of the thermometers in the plastic bag and tie the bag so it is airtight.
2. Put the bag in direct sunlight for about 10 minutes.
3. Put the other thermometer beside the bag.
4. Wait for about 15 minutes and then look at the two temperatures. What do you notice?

Materials
- 2 thermometers
- clear plastic bag

Did You Know?

When the sunlight travels into the plastic bag the light turns into heat. The inside of the bag gets hotter because the air can't escape quickly enough. The sunlight does the same thing when it enters Earth's atmosphere. This is called the greenhouse effect.

316 Tracking the Sun

What happens to the Sun when the Earth moves?

STEPS

1. Tape the piece of paper to the floor in front of a window the sun shines through.
2. Draw a line with the marker exactly where the sunlight's edge appears on the floor as it shines through the window. Write the date and the time beside the line.
3. Each week, at exactly the same time, mark the sunlight's edge on the paper and record the date.
4. Continue marking the sunlight's edge until you run out of paper. What do you notice?

Materials
- large piece of paper 40 in (100 cm) long
- tape
- marker

Did You Know?
The Earth moves around the Sun.

---

317 Thirsty Dish

See how much water evaporates in 24 hours.

STEPS

1. Put water in the dish.
2. Put the dish on the scales and write down its weight. Leave the dish uncovered for one day.
3. Look at the scales. Has the weight changed? It should weigh less because water has evaporated into the air—it is not being swallowed by the dish!

Materials
- kitchen scales
- dish
- water

Did You Know?
Evaporation is an important part of the water cycle. The water in the air rises up to the clouds and returns back to the Earth as rain.

318 Bags of Wind

Materials
- plastic bag

Find out which direction the wind is blowing.

STEPS

1. Go outside on a windy day.
2. Hold the handles of the plastic bag in each hand. The wind will fill the bag with air and blow the bag in the same direction as the wind.

Did You Know?
Windsocks are used to help pilots note the wind direction and take this into account when landing their planes.

---

319 Flying High

Materials
- flag or towel
- compass
- clothespins

Find out the direction of the wind (north, south, east, or west).

STEPS

1. Pin the flag or towel to the washing line.
2. Observe the direction the wind is blowing the flag.
3. Use the compass to work out from which direction the wind is blowing.

A southern breeze! Just what Mom needs to dry the washing. I'm sure she'll want to put on another load!

Did You Know?
We have air pressure pushing on our bodies all the time. It's actually about 14 lb (6 kg) of air pressure!

320 Cool as Water or Air?

See if air or water holds more heat.

STEPS

1. Place both of the glasses in the freezer.
2. Take them out of the freezer after 10 minutes. Which glass feels warmer?

Materials
- 2 glasses, one filled with water and one empty (filled with air)
- freezer

Did You Know?

The glass with the water in it feels warmer because the empty glass, which is really full of air, lost its heat much more quickly than the water lost its heat. So we know water holds more heat than air!

321 Make Your Own Air Pressure

Can you create your own air pressure?

Materials
- funnel
- ping pong ball

STEPS

1. Put the ping pong ball inside the funnel.
2. Tilt your head back and blow air into the funnel. Try to blow the ping pong ball out of the funnel. What happens?

Did You Know?

The fast rushing air travels around the edges of the ball, rather than just pushing it straight up!

322 Indoor Clouds

Materials
- tea kettle filled with water
- metal tray

Make your own cloud.

STEPS

1. Ask for help to boil the water in the tea kettle.
2. As the water boils and steam begins to appear, place the tray above the spout. Droplets of water will begin to appear on the tray. These tiny droplets of water are what clouds are made of.

Did You Know?

Clouds are formed when the Sun heats the air around us, which then rises up into the sky. Eventually, the warm air gets colder until it turns into tiny drops of water or ice. Millions of these droplets cling together to form the clouds we can see. Once the droplets get too heavy, they fall back down to Earth as rain or snow.

---

323 My Own Puddle

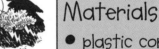

Materials
- plastic container (an old takeout food container would be perfect)
- measuring cup
- pen
- paper

See how long it takes for a small puddle to evaporate.

STEPS

1. Make a hole in the ground and place the plastic container in it. If you don't have a yard, put the container on a windowsill.
2. Measure one cup of water and pour it into your bowl.
3. Record the day on your piece of paper.
4. Observe the container each day until all of the water has evaporated. How long did it take?

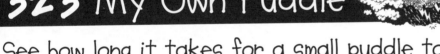

Did You Know?

When water evaporates it becomes invisible.

324 Make Your Own Frost

See how frost forms.

STEPS

1. Crush two cups of ice and put it in the can.
2. Add half a cup of rock salt.
3. Stir the ice and rock salt rapidly.
4. Leave the mixture for half an hour.
5. After half an hour the can will have some dew on it.
6. If you wait a bit longer, the dew will turn into frost.

Materials
- rock salt
- crushed ice
- can without a lid

Did You Know?
There is moisture in the air we breathe. As the can gets colder the moisture in the air condenses on its surface. This is why the dew on the can turned to frost. Just like frost on the grass on a very cold morning!

325 Patterns in the Frost

See how frost forms and makes patterns.

STEPS

1. Pour the crushed ice and rock salt into the can.
2. Stir it together quickly.
3. Slightly moisten the paper cut-outs and place them around the outside of the can.
4. Leave the can for about half an hour. Dew will begin to form on the outside of the can, and if you leave it for a bit longer the dew will turn into frost.
5. Peel off the paper cut-outs and look at the patterns you have made!

Materials
- a clean can
- ½ cup of rock salt
- 1 cup of crushed ice
- spoon small paper cut-outs of different shapes

Did You Know?
As the can cools down, the air molecules cool down and close in on the water (dew) outside it. The water (dew) gets cooler and frost forms.

326 Transported By Air

Find out some of the things that can be carried by the wind.

STEPS

1. Take the piece of cardboard and put a hole in the top of it using the scissors.
2. Thread the string through the hole and tie it on.
3. Paint one side of the cardboard with the glue.
4. Hang the piece of cardboard outside for about an hour (longer if it is not a windy day).
5. Look at what is stuck to the cardboard and see what the wind has been carrying!

There I was, just flying around the yard, minding my own business when someone sticks a piece of sticky cardboard in my way.

Materials
- glue made from flour and water
- cardboard about 13.9 × 19.7 in (35 × 50 cm)
- string
- scissors
- paintbrush

Did You Know?
The wind carries seeds from plants and spreads them around to new places.

---

327 Air, Air Everywhere

Air is everywhere, even though we can't see it.

STEPS

1. Put the plastic bottle into the bucket of water until it is completely covered with water and gently squeeze. Bubbles will come out of the bottle, which shows us that while the bottle appeared to be empty, it was actually full of air!

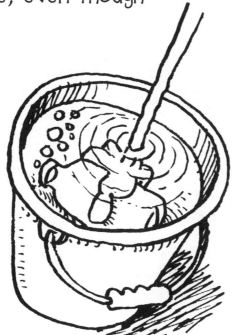

Materials
- bucket of water
- plastic bottle

Did You Know?
Wind is moving air, and something has to make it move. Take a deep breath and then breathe out. Your body is making that air into wind!

328 Make Your Own Cloud

See how clouds form.

STEPS

1. Pour a little bit of warm water into the bottle, just enough to cover the bottom.
2. Ask for help to light the match and let it burn for a little while.
3. Blow the match out and immediately let the smoke from the match fill the bottle. The smoke will clear quite quickly, but there will be invisible particles floating in the bottle.
4. Screw the cap onto the bottle and try to keep as much smoke in the bottle as you can.
5. Squeeze the bottle six or seven times.

Materials
- a clear plastic bottle with a cap
- warm water
- matches

Did You Know?
Fluffy clouds are called cumulus clouds.

---

329 Flouring Rain

Observe the 3D shape of rain drops.

STEPS

1. Put one cup of flour into the bowl.
2. Either put the bowl outside in the rain for five minutes then bring it back inside, or drip about five drops of water from the eye dropper into the flour.
3. Leave it to stand for about five minutes.
4. Sift the flour gently, allowing the loose flour to fall through to the plate.
5. The flour rain drops should be left in the sieve.
6. Gently place them on a piece of paper. Are they the same size and shape?

Materials
- bowl
- flour
- sieve
- plate
- rain (an eyedropper will work too)
- water

Did You Know?
Mawsynram, India, is reported to be the wettest place on Earth, with around 470 in (12 m) of rainfall per year.

330 Measuring Thunder

See how long it takes to hear the sound of thunder.

STEPS

1. Go to a safe, dry place in your house where you can see outside.

2. Watch for a flash of lightning. As soon as you see the lightning, start the stopwatch. When you hear the thunder, stop the stopwatch.

3. For every five seconds the storm is 1 mile (1.6 km) away. So …
   5 seconds: 1 mile
   10 seconds: 2 miles
   15 seconds: 3 miles
   20 seconds: 4 miles etc.

Materials
- thunderstorm
- stopwatch

My, it is a stormy day! I seem to be generating enough lightning of my own, but I must stick to measuring the lightning outside.

Did You Know?
If you see lightning without thunder following it, the lightning is more than 15 miles (24 km) away, which is too far away for you to hear the sound of the thunder.

331 Flying Kites

Does the wind push or pull a kite?

STEPS

1. Go outside to a place where you can run with your kite.

2. Feel which way the wind is blowing. Try to fly your kite the same way the wind is blowing.

3. Now run into the wind so you feel the wind blowing in your face. Which way did the kite fly best?

Materials
- kite
- windy day

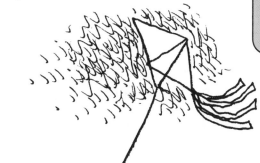

Did You Know?
Earth's rotation affects the direction the wind blows!

332 Slippery Skin

Materials
- small coin
- water

Find out where air pressure can be found.

STEPS

1. Press the coin onto your cheek. It falls off quite easily.
2. Put a little bit of water on one side of the coin.
3. Place the damp side of the coin on your cheek.

Whoops! If I had a real cheek that coin would stick, but I'm all water! Sorry!

Did You Know?
Air is pressing all over the coin and when you add water to the coin it pushes out the air between the coin and your skin.

333 Popping Air!

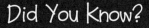

Materials
- empty coffee can (with a lid)
- very hot water

See the effect of air pressure when the air gets hot.

STEPS

1. Ask for help to pour the hot water into the can.
2. Put the lid on the can.
3. Stand back (do not have your face close to the can) and watch what happens. The lid will fly off. This is because the air inside the can is getting warmer and it is expanding.

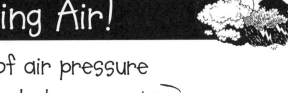

Did You Know?
When air is heated it expands and increases the air pressure!

334 The Pressing Issue of Air

See what happens when water replaces air.

Materials
- water
- coins

STEPS

1. Rub two coins together. They should rub very easily.
2. Put water between the two coins and try rubbing them together now. Do they rub easily?

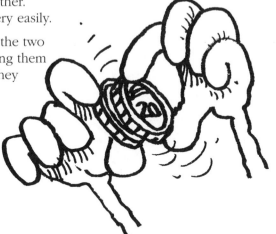

Did You Know?

Air presses on the coins and when the water is put between the coins it replaces the air between them. This stops the coins from moving together easily.

335 Tornado in a Bottle!

See how a tornado moves.

Materials
- 1 clear plastic bottle
- 5 small aluminum foil balls
- water
- blue food dye
- teaspoon
- clear liquid soap

STEPS

1. Measure one teaspoon of the liquid soap and pour it into the bottle.
2. Drop the foil balls into the bottle.
3. Fill the bottle with water.
4. Add a couple of drops of blue food dye.
5. Rotate the bottle and you should see a swirling motion. The swirling represents the motion of a tornado.

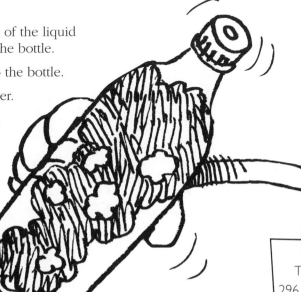

Did You Know?

The fastest tornado winds recorded, 296 miles (476 km) per hour, happened in 2013, in El Reno, Oklahoma.

336 Watery Air

See water in the air.

STEPS

1. Put a dry glass (upside down) under a running (cold water) faucet. Keep the inside of the glass dry. This will make the glass cold.
2. Take the glass out from under the faucet, and breathe heavily into the glass. A thin lining of water drops should form inside the glass. This water was in your breath.

Materials
- drinking glass
- water

Did You Know?
When rain falls from the clouds it is because the water droplets have become too heavy!

337 Hot or Cold Balloons?

See the effect temperature has on balloons.

STEPS

1. Blow the two balloons up to much the same size.
2. Use the marker to mark one with "H" (for hot) and one with "C" (for cold).
3. Put the "C" balloon in the freezer (or refrigerator).
4. Put the "H" balloon in the box.
5. Gently blow warm air from the hair dryer into the box.
6. After about 10 minutes compare the balloons. What has happened?

Materials
- 2 balloons
- hair dryer
- box (a cardboard box with a lid is good)
- freezer (or refrigerator)
- marker

Did You Know?
Hot air expands and cool air contracts!

338 Air is in the Atmosphere

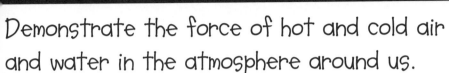

Demonstrate the force of hot and cold air and water in the atmosphere around us.

STEPS

1. Ask for help to fill about one-third of the plastic bottle with very hot water (not boiling because the plastic will melt!).
2. Put the lid on the bottle.
3. Fill the large bowl with cold water and ice.
4. Put the plastic bottle in the bowl and make sure it is covered with the cool water and ice. What has happened to the bottle?

Did You Know?

The pressure of the air inside the bottle is not as great as the pressure in the atmosphere, which means the air pressure on the outside of the bottle crushes it!

Materials
- funnel
- hot water
- cold water
- large bowl
- plastic soda bottle
- ice

339 Umbrellas!

How important is waterproof fabric?

STEPS

1. Put up both umbrellas.
2. Sprinkle some water on the real umbrella. What do you notice happens to the water?
3. Sprinkle some water on the small paper umbrella. What do you notice happens to the water? The water on the real umbrella rolls down the side, whereas water on the small paper umbrella is absorbed.

Materials
- real umbrella
- small paper umbrella (used as decoration in drinks)
- water

Did You Know?

Umbrellas that keep the sun off your skin are called parasols. These are not made from waterproof fabric.

340 In the Heat of the Sun

Feel some of the heat of the Sun.

STEPS

1. Keep the blind or curtain drawn. Put your hand up to the glass. Can you feel any heat?

2. Put the blind or curtain up. Put your hand up to the glass. Can you feel any heat now? What happened?

Materials
- a window with a blind or curtain

Did You Know?
The Sun is a star that is 93 million miles (149.6 million km) away!

341 Evaporation

See how water evaporates.

STEPS

1. Half fill the cups with water.
2. Add food dye to one of the cups.
3. Use the eye dropper to get the clear water from one cup and drop a couple of drops onto the paper towel.
4. Use the eye dropper to get the dyed water from one cup and drop a couple of drops onto the paper towel.
5. Keep a watchful eye on the paper towel and observe what happens. The water will evaporate from the towel, leaving the food dye behind, but nothing will be left behind from the clear water droplets.

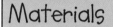

Materials
- 2 cups
- food dye
- eye dropper
- paper towel

Did You Know?
Evaporation is how water becomes tiny droplets that form the clouds!

342 Raining at Sea

See what might happen to a tin boat when it rains.

STEPS

1. Fill the bucket with water.
2. Make the empty plastic cup float on the water in the bucket.
3. Slowly sprinkle water from the watering can into the plastic cup. What is happening to the plastic cup?

Of all the places to be caught out in a terrible storm! A plastic bucket!

Materials
- plastic cup (to act as a tin boat)
- bucket of water (to act as a lake or ocean)
- watering can (to act as the rain)

Did You Know?
Clouds change shape because as they come into contact with warm air, parts of them evaporate. As clouds come into contact with cold air, raindrops form and fall.

---

343 Puddles of Hail

See what happens when ice melts.

STEPS

1. Fill the plastic cup three-quarters full with water.
2. Put the ice cube in the cup of water. What do you think will happen as the ice cube melts?

Materials
- small ice cube (to act as hail)
- plastic cup (to act as the puddle)

Did You Know?
Hailstones have been known to be the size of golf balls!

344 The Fading Sun

See some of the effects of the heat from the Sun.

STEPS

1. Lay a piece of newspaper down outside in direct sunlight using a paper weight to keep it still.
2. Lay a piece of newspaper down inside, out of the sunlight, using a paper weight to keep it still.
3. Leave the newspapers in their positions for one week.
4. After a week, compare the two pieces of newspaper. What has happened to the paper?

Materials
- 2 pieces of newspaper
- 2 paper weights

Did You Know?
During winter, the Sun is 90 million miles (145 million km) away from Earth.

---

345 Classifying Clouds

Observe different types of clouds.

STEPS

1. Go outside on a cloudy day and observe the clouds in the sky.
2. Identify the types of clouds that are in the sky from the list below.
3. Draw the clouds you can see.

- Cirrus are white and feathery (the highest clouds).
- Cumulus are puffy clouds that look like cotton balls.
- Stratus are flat, wide looking clouds (drizzle usually falls from these clouds).
- Nimbus are dark, gray rainy clouds.

4. You can observe clouds over a few days and comment on the similarities and differences. The weather will influence the types of clouds in the sky.

Materials
- clouds
- paper
- pencils

Did You Know?
Clouds are fog in the sky!

346 Underwater Clouds

Observe the difference in the density of hot and cold water.

STEPS

1. Pour cold water into the large glass bowl until it is three-quarters full.
2. Fill the jar with hot water—not hot enough to burn your fingers though.
3. Drip a few drops of the food dye into the jar.
4. Put the lid on the jar and shake it so the water and the food dye mix.
5. Put the jar into the glass bowl full of cold water.
6. Wait for the water to settle.
7. Put your hands in the water and very gently undo the lid of the jar and remove it. Be very careful to try not to move the water.
8. Gently take your hands out of the water. What happens?

Materials
- large clear bowl (or a glass vase)
- cold water (from the refrigerator)
- small glass jar with a lid
- food dye

Did You Know?
The sea contains 97 percent of Earth's water.

347 Making an Eye Dropper

Observe the pressure of air and water.

STEPS

1. Suck up some of the water through the straw.
2. Cover the end of the straw with your finger (usually the end you have been sucking from, but it works as well if you cover the other end).
3. Lift your finger off the straw for a second, then quickly replace it. Each time you lift your finger from the straw some water will be released.

Materials
- drinking straw
- water

Did You Know?
The more experiments you do, the better you will get at releasing one small drop.

348 Walking Water

Observe the movement of water through a paper towel.

STEPS

1. Fill one of the cups with water.
2. Place the cup full of water on top of the upside down bowl (or something that will raise the cup).
3. Place one end of the paper towel in the cup with water, making sure it is touching the bottom of the cup.
4. Put the other end of the paper towel in the other cup. What happens?
5. Repeat the experiment, but this time change the width of the piece of paper towel.

Materials
- water
- 2 clear plastic cups
- paper towel, cut into strips
- bowl

Did You Know?
Paper has many tiny spaces. The water fills these tiny spaces and moves along the paper.

349 Absorbing Water Drops

Discover what sort of objects absorb water.

STEPS

1. Place all of the items in a row, outside or in the bathtub.
2. With your watering can or sieve gently pour the "rain" over the different objects. Which objects absorbed the water? Which objects didn't absorb the water? Why didn't they all absorb the water?

Did You Know?
Objects that absorb water are called porous, which means they have lots of tiny holes.

Materials
- paper towel
- glossy magazine page
- aluminum foil
- cardboard
- wood
- plastic
- water
- watering can or a sieve

350 Bubbles of Rainbows

See the different colors made by rainbows.

STEPS

1. Put one teaspoon of sugar into the bubble mix.
2. Put the mix into the fridge (it helps the bubbles last longer).
3. Dip the blower into the mixture.
4. Gently blow a bubble and try not to it let fly away.
5. Attach the bubble to the bubble stand. Wait a little while and you will be able to see different colors in the bubble!

Did You Know?

In Australia, Darwin in the Northern Territory is the sunniest city. It has an average of 8.5 hours of sunshine a day, whereas Melbourne in Victoria has the dubious honor of being Australia's least sunny city, with an average of 5.7 hours of sunshine each day.

Materials
- bubble mix
- (dishwashing detergent works well too)
- teaspoon
- sugar
- bubble blower
- refrigerator
- bubble stand (an upside down plastic cup will work! It will work even better if coated with bubble mix)

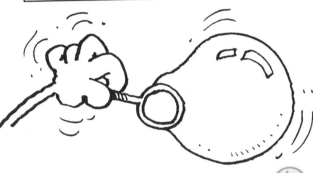

---

351 Picture Snowflakes

Make a snowflake picture.

STEPS

1. On your computer, type the word "snowflake" into Google.
2. Choose an option about snowflakes.
3. Look at the patterns. What do you notice about them?
4. Use your imagination to draw some snowflakes of your own.

Materials
- computer
- pencil
- sheet of paper

Did You Know?

Snowflakes all have six sides (hexagonal) and are symmetrical. Every one of the countless billions that fall is different, so you can never run out of snowflake patterns to draw!

352 Wind Force

Observe the force of wind.

Materials
- plastic bottle
- small piece of paper rolled up into the size of a pea

STEPS

1. Put the bottle on its side on a table or bench.
2. Put the paper in the neck of the bottle.
3. Blow hard and fast into the bottle. What happens to the piece of paper? (The fast moving air should go straight past the piece of paper, hit the back of the bottle, and then come out again, forcing the little ball of paper to come out!)

Did You Know?

The windiest place in the world is Port Martin, Antarctica, which has an average wind speed over a year of 40 mph (64 km/h). It experiences gale force 8 winds for over a hundred days a year!

353 Wind Watching

Can a strong wind affect the outcome of a ball game?

Materials
- ball

STEPS

1. Go outside and throw the ball the same way the wind is blowing. The wind will help the ball to travel farther.
2. This time throw the ball against the wind. The wind pushes against the ball and the ball will not travel as far.

Did You Know?

In Australia hurricanes are sometimes called "Willy Willies."

354 Sunlight Spotlight

See how the Sun's rays are reflected.

STEPS

1. Cover the cardboard squares with the foil, shiny side up.
2. Find a stream of sunshine.
3. Put the foil in the path of the sunshine, and then reflect the sun in the direction you would like it to go. The reflection can then act as a spotlight!

Materials
- cardboard squares
- aluminum foil
- sunshine

Did You Know?
You should not stay in the Sun for too long because the Sun damages your skin even when it does not feel that hot.

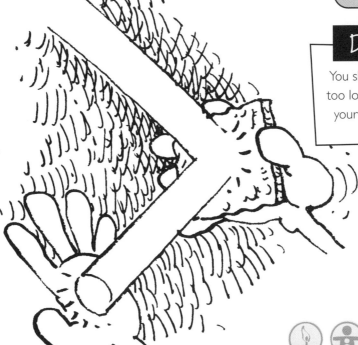

---

355 Water Paintings

Learn more about the water cycle.

STEPS

1. Wet the paintbrush with water.
2. Paint a picture using the water as "paint." When you have finished, leave your water painting for a few hours. What happens?

Materials
- paintbrush
- water
- dry surface, such as concrete or asphalt

Did You Know?
The heat from the Sun causes the water from your painting to evaporate. It then turns into water vapor and heads back up to the clouds!

356 Dyed Ice

See how color is affected by heat.

Materials
- ice-cube tray
- food dye
- water
- freezer

STEPS

1. Fill the ice-cube tray with water.
2. In each section of the tray, drip one or two drops of food dye—make sure you leave one with just plain water.
3. In one section drip in many different dyes in order to make the ice cube as dark as possible.
4. Put the ice-cube tray in the freezer and leave it to freeze.
5. Take the ice cubes out and watch them melt. What do you notice? (The darkest ice cube should melt the quickest!)

Did You Know?
The heaviest hailstone that has ever been recorded fell on April 14, 1986 in Bangladesh. It weighed 2.25 lb (1 kg).

357 Heavy Air

Demonstrate that there is air pressure all around us.

Materials
- folded sheet of newspaper
- old 12 in (30 cm) wooden ruler or flat stick
- counter

STEPS

1. Put the ruler on the bench with about a quarter of it hanging out over the edge. Be careful here!
2. Carefully, with your head and body back, give the end of the ruler that is hanging over the edge a karate chop. (The ruler will go flying!)
3. Retrieve the ruler and set it up the same way as in step 1.
4. Now put the newspaper over the part of the ruler that is on the bench, leaving the overhanging section uncovered.
5. Give the ruler another karate chop. What happened this time? (The air pressure on top of the newspaper should be so great that it snaps the ruler!)

Did You Know?
The air is pushing down on the folded sheet of newspaper so hard that it weighs more than 1.1 tons (1 metric ton)!

358 Wet and Dry

Feel the difference between wet and dry clothing.

STEPS

1. Put the socks on your feet.
2. Put one foot in the bucket of water, and keep the other sock/foot dry. How do your feet feel? Your wet foot should feel much colder than your dry foot. The dry foot is surrounded by air, and the wet foot is surrounded by water because it has pushed the air away.

Materials
- pair of socks
- bucket
- water

Did You Know?
Water can take on many different forms, such as liquid, solid, or gas.

---

359 Heater or Refrigerator?

Feel the difference between cool air and warm air.

STEPS

1. Stand in front of your radiator for a few minutes.
2. Stand in front of your open fridge for a few moments. When you stand in front of the radiator you feel warm air and when you stand in front of the refrigerator you feel cold air.

Materials
- radiator
- refrigerator

Did You Know?
Hot air balloons were invented in France in 1783. Type "hot air balloon" into Google on your computer and read the history of this method of transport.

360 Daze in the Clouds

How do humidity, temperature, and air pressure influence the way clouds are formed?

STEPS

1. Measure ½ fl oz (15 mL) of water and tip it into the jar.
2. Put the lit match into the jar. Ask for help to do this.
3. Put the plastic bag over the jar as fast as you can and use the rubber band to secure it to the jar.
4. Push the bag into the jar.
5. Now pull the bag out of the jar. When you push the bag into the jar the pressure and the temperature in the jar go up, and make the jar look clear. When you pull the bag out, the pressure and the temperature go down, so then the water vapor condenses, which makes the cloud in the jar.

Materials
- large glass jar
- rubber band
- clear plastic bag
- water
- matches
- measuring cup
- water

Did You Know?
Vapor is the name for invisible, evaporated water.

361 Precipitation

See how precipitation forms.

STEPS

1. Pour one cup of hot water into the jar. (You may need to ask an adult to help you do this.)
2. Put the funnel in the jar.
3. Now put the plastic bag into the funnel.
4. Pour the cold water into the plastic bag and add the ice cubes. Watch the jar. What is happening?

Materials
- funnel
- plastic bag
- jar
- 1 cup hot tap water
- ¼ cup cold water
- ice cubes

Did You Know?
The world's water cycle is never ending. It travels on a journey from the sky to the land or sea and travels back up to the clouds again!

362 Color and the Weather

What are some of the principles of solar power?

STEPS

1. Spread the piece of newspaper outside in the Sun.
2. Place the different colored squares on the newspaper.
3. Place an ice cube on each piece of paper.
4. Time how long it takes each ice cube to melt. What do you notice?

Materials
- 6 pieces of colored paper about 4 in × 4 in (10 cm × 10 cm)
- 6 ice cubes
- newspaper
- clock

Did You Know?
Dark colors absorb heat and light, and light colors reflect heat and light.

---

363 Salty Rain

Why doesn't salt water become salt rain?

STEPS

1. Taste the water (make sure it's not too hot to drink).
2. Add the salt to the water and stir it to help the salt dissolve. Taste the water now.
3. Place the salty water into the pan. Now ask an adult to help you boil the water on the stove. Keep the lid on.
4. Condensation will form on the lid. As it does, take the lid off and let the water drip off the lid into the cup.
5. When the water in the cup cools down, taste it. How does it taste?

Materials
- 2 teaspoons of salt
- 2 cups warm water
- stove
- spoon
- pan with a lid
- cup

Did You Know?
The water from the sea gets heated by the sun, evaporates to form water vapor, and eventually becomes salt-less water in the clouds.

364 Freezing Liquids

Find out about freezing different liquids.

STEPS

1. Fill one ice-cube tray with water.
2. Fill one ice-cube tray with vinegar.
3. Fill one ice-cube tray with cooking oil.
4. Put the ice-cube tray into the freezer.
5. Record what time you put the tray in the freezer. Check the tray every hour and write down your findings. The water freezes into a hard block; the vinegar should freeze too; but what happens to the oil?

Materials
- ice-cube tray
- vinegar
- water
- cooking oil
- freezer

Did You Know?
The world's largest known iceberg was 183 miles (295 km) long!

365 Water—Putting on Weight!

See how much water expands when it freezes.

STEPS

1. Fill the bowl with water.
2. Put the film canister in the water and fill it with water. Make sure there aren't any air bubbles, then put the lid on.
3. Take the film canister out of the water and put it in the snap-lock bag.
4. Put the snap-lock bag in the freezer for 24 hours. What happens to the film canister?

Materials
- film canister with a lid
- water
- freezer
- Zip-lock bag
- bowl

Did You Know?
When frozen, water expands by about 9–10 percent.

Notes

Index

A

Absorbing Water Drops	349
Acid or Base?	145
A Home-made Seismograph	233
A Home-made Stethoscope	239
Air, Air Everywhere	327
Air is in the Atmosphere	338
Aliens in the Night	53
A Magnet Can be a Compass	298
Am I Upside Down?	254
Angled Light	12
Animal Activities	118
A Sedimentary Situation	225
Astronaut Suits	57
At-home Paleontologist	186
At-home Volcano	193
Attracting Butterflies	104
Avalanche!	229

B

Bags of Wind	318
Baked Ice Cream	159
Balloon Rocket	48
Balloon Static	292
Bark Detective	82
Bark Rubbing	81
Barney Banana	71
Bedroom Nights	35
Biodegradable Bags	220
Bird Beaks	116
Bird Calls	114
Black Holes	27
Blowing Bubbles	172
Bounce!	274
Bounce Factors	276
Bounce Higher!	275
Breathing Plants	66
Brown Apples	142
Brown Light? Clear Light?	93
Bubble Rocket	49
Bubbles of Rainbows	350
Bubbly Drink	173
Buzzy Bees	99

C

Candy Dissolving	165
Carbon Everywhere	125
Catching Ants	100
Catching Rain Drops	304
Catch Me, I'm Falling!	273
Ceiling Rainbows	251
Centrifugal Force	50
Chalk Talk	214
Changing Shape	126
Classifying Clouds	345
Classifying Living Things	63
Clean Cleaner	146
Clean Money	147
Climbing Colors	151
Color and the Weather	362
Color Your Life	252
Colorful Sugar	127
Combing the Shadows	259
Compost is My Home	78
Conduction	128
Cool as Water or Air?	320
Cooling Down	129
Corny Goo	130
Crater Than Thou	272
Crazy Leaves	84
Create a New Insect	102
Creating an Eclipse	13
Crystal on a String	208
Crystals Everywhere	150
Crystal Star	149

D

Day and Night	8
Daze in the Clouds	360
Demagnetize Me	301
Design a Beak for You!	117
Different Moons	18
Digging for Dinosaurs	188
Disappearing Act	148
Dishing up the Crystals	207
Diving Raisins	174
Don't Sink the Boat	291
Double Balloon Static	290
Double Magnetism	300
Down with Gravity	5
Dyed Ice	356

E

E.T. Rocks	43
Eating in Space	56
Eggs Continental	223
Evaporation	341

F

Falling Over	271
Fast Rust	132
Feeding the Birds	110
Feelin' the Pressure	270
Feeling a Little Tense?	269
Filter Fun	257
Finding Your Bearings	62
Fire Extinguisher	175
Fizzin' Minerals	210
Fizzy Sherbet	177
Float or Sink?	197
Flouring Rain	329
Flying High	319
Flying in Space	59
Flying Kites	331
Footprint Detectives	120
Footprints	121
Freezing Cold—Part A	306
Freezing Cold—Part B	307
Freezing Liquids	364
Fruit or Vegetable?	72
Funny Funnel	267
Fun to Spin	268

G

Gas to Liquid	152
Gazing at Stars	25
Grass Heads	97
Grasses	80
Gravity	2
Gravity Pulls	3
Greenhouse Effect	38
Green Slime	131
Green to Red	178
Growing Both Ends	65
Guard Dogs	119
Gumdrop Molecules	123

H

Hangin' Out For Answers	279
Hard and Soft Water	153
Heater or Refrigerator?	359
Heat is in the Air	314
Heavy Air	357
Hey, I'm Eroding Away!	222
Hey, You're Blocking My Funnel!	215
Home-made Geodes	204
Home-made Glue	154
Hot or Cold Balloons?	337
How Heavy is the Air?	313
How Old Are You Really?	36
How Slow Is a Snail?	106
How Strong is a Snail?	107
How to Make a Parachute	277

I

Images of the Sun	14
Indoor Clouds	322
In the Heat of the Sun	340
Invisible Ink	155
Is a Spider an Insect?	98
Is That Egg Hard-boiled?	171
I've Found It!	255

J

Jar Compass	238
Journey to the Middle of the Earth	218
Jumping Up	287

L

Lava Icing	196
Leaf Eaters	103
Leaf Rubbing	83
Lemon Floaties	75
Lifting Higher	284
Lights Out	176
Like Them Lemons?	289
Living in Ice	308
Lost My Marbles	283

M

Magic Balloon	70
Magic Floating Objects	282
Magnetic Field	299
Magnetic Rocks	205
Make an Ant Colony	101
Make Your Own Air Pressure	321
Make Your Own Cloud	328
Make Your Own Frost	324
Make Your Own Lightning	311
Make Your Own Thunder	310
Making a Birdbath	113
Making a Bird Caller	115
Making a Bird Feeder	111
Making a Butterfly	105
Making a Compost Bin	77
Making a Siphon	280
Making a Spiral Galaxy	30
Making an Eye Dropper	347
Making Conglomerate Rock	185
Making Ginger Ale	74
Making Gravity	4
Making Limestone	184
Making Mountains Last	221
Making Pet Rocks	212
Making Pot-pourri	87
Making Rivers	231
Making Sandstone	182
Making Starch	124
Making the Distance	244
Mapping It Out	235
Mapping the Ocean Floor	227
Matchbox Cars	297
Materials and Their Uses	133
Measuring Temperature	303
Measuring Thunder	330
Melting Ice	157
Melting Ice Hands-free	286
Melting Polar Ice Caps	219
Melting Salty Ice	309
Melt or Burn?	134
Metamorphic Pancakes	203
Meteor Burnout	45
Meteorites & Craters	44
Mighty Whites	253
Milky Plastic	144
Minerals, Minerals Everywhere	211
Mini Greenhouse	68
Missing Footprints	187
Mold Mania	76
Moon Gazing	20
Musical Bottles	245
Musical Wine Glasses	243
My Crust is Bent!	224
My Magnetic House	293
My Own Plane Wing	281
My Own Puddle	323

N

Need Your Lenses Fixed?	249
North Pole or South Pole?	296

O

Observing Birds Feeding	112
Observing Night and Day	9
Opposites Attract	295
Orbiting Satellites	61
Orbiting the Sun	39
Our Solar System	41

P

Pangaea: The Ancient Continent	181
Patterns in the Frost	325
Peppery Skin	161
Phases of the Moon	19
Picture Snowflakes	351
Plants and Air	90
Plants and Soil	91
Plants and Water	92
Plants From Other Plants	95
Play-doh Mountains	232
Pond in a Jar	109
Popping Air!	333
Potato Asteroids	37
Precipitation	361
Preserving Food	135
Pressed Leaves & Flowers	86
Pretend Panning	216
Puddles of Hail	343
Purple Celery	88

R

Rainbow in Your Hand	256
Rainbow Light	250
Raining at Sea	342
Reflective Telescopes	22
Refracting Telescopes	23
Reverse	248
Rise Up	122
Robot Arms	52
Rocket Launch	46
Rock Hunt	192
Rock or Not!	217
Rock Search	191
Rocork Launch!	47
Rubbery Egg	143
Rubbing the Glacial Way	202
Rusty Mars	40

S

Sailing the High Seas	265
Salty Bean Sprouts	96
Salty Ice	158
Salty Rain	363
Save Our Chemicals!	137
Seasons	10
Seeing Ions in Action	288
See Inside a Box	6
Settle Down, Pencil!	234
Shadow Dances	54
Signals and Satellites	60
Slidin' Mudslides	230
Slippery Leaves	67
Slippery Skin	332
Slippery Snake	294
Smell That Gas	179
Smog Alert	237
Snappy Ruler	242
Soap Boats	162
Soil Search	189
Sorting Materials	138
Space Clouds	32
Speeding Stars	31
Splitting Light	29
Squishy Ice cream	160
Stalagmite or Stalactite?	209
Standing in the Shadows	247
Star Gazers	34
Star Gazing	28
Star Motion	26

Stars in the Day	24
Stem-less Flowers	89
Stickin' to the Outline	246
Stretchy Stockings	139
Sunlight Spotlight	354
Sunset in a Box	17
Sunspots	15
Super Hearing	58
Sweating Plants	69
Sweaty Eggplants	156
Swirly Patterns	163

T

Tall or Short?	180
That's Volcanic!	195
The Amazing Floating Rock	199
The Amazing Jumping Men	302
The Big Freeze	169
The Big Ice	170
The Boxing Kangaroos	285
The Fading Sun	344
The Floating Egg	136
The Matchbox Guitar	241
The Moving Sun	16
The Oldest Tree	79
The Pressing Issue of Air	334
The Shape of Earth	7
The Shape of Rain Drops	305
The Slow-moving Glacier	201
The Sun and Us	1
The Swing of Things	278
The Thirsty Brick	183
The Tides	11
Thirsty Dish	317
This is Very Hard!	206
Tilted Bottle	166
Tornado in a Bottle!	335
Tracking the Sun	316
Transported By Air	326
Travel to the Moon	55
Tree Encyclopedia	85
Turning Inside a Balloon	264
Turning to White	258

U

Umbrellas!	339
Undercover Leaves	94
Underwater Clouds	346
Unusual Pendulum	263
Uranus and the Sun	42

V

Volcanic "Mud"	200
Volcano in the Sandpile!	194
Volume	167

W

Walking Water	348
Wall of Water	236
Watch Out for the Quicksand	226
Watch This!	262
Water Paintings	355
Water—Putting on Weight!	365
Watery Air	336
Wax Factor	164
Wet and Dry	358
What Is It?	140
What is the Greenhouse Effect?	315
What's in Dirt?	190
What's in Sand?	213
What's That Noise?	240
When is a Fruit a Berry?	73
Which Parachute?	261
Which Rock is the Thirstiest?	198
Who's Got the Fastest Car?	260
Will Humpty-Dumpty Crack?	266
Will It Mix?	168
Wind Force	352
Wind Watching	353
Withered Potatoes	64
Wondrous Woodchips	228
Working in Space	51
Wriggling Worms	108
Wrinkly Apple	141

Y

Your Own Hurricane!	312
Your Own Quadrant	33
Your Weight on the Moon	21

Published by Hinkler Pty Ltd
45–55 Fairchild Street
Heatherton Victoria 3202 Australia
www.hinkler.com.au

hinkler

Text, Cover Design © Hinkler Pty Ltd 2007, 2010, 2014, 2021
Design © Hinkler Pty Ltd 2007, 2014, 2021

Editor: Estelle Longfield
Illustrations: Glen Singleton
Design and Art Direction: Katy Wall
Typesetting: Palmer Higgs and Macmillan Publishing Solutions
Translation into American English by Tall Tree Ltd

Cover image: © Shutterstock, whanwhan.ai

2 4 6 8 10 9 7 5 3
11 13 15 14 12

All rights reserved. No part of this publication may be reproduced, stored in a retrieval system, or transmitted in any way or by any means, electronic, mechanical, photocopying, recording or otherwise, without the prior written permission of Hinkler Books Pty Ltd.

ISBN: 978 1 4889 4571 7

Printed and bound in China